Daddy's *Delight*

Daddy's *Delight*

Embracing
Your
DIVINE
DESIGN

KARIA BUNTING

MOODY PUBLISHERS
CHICAGO

All Scripture quotations, unless otherwise indicated, are taken from the *New American Standard Bible*®, Copyright © 1960, 1962, 1963, 1968, 1971, 1972, 1973, 1975, 1977, 1995 by The Lockman Foundation. Used by permission. (www.Lockman.org)

Scripture quotations marked KJV are taken from the King James Version.

Scripture quotations marked THE MESSAGE are from *The Message*, copyright © by Eugene H. Peterson 1993, 1994, 1995. Used by permission of NavPress Publishing Group.

Edited by Kathryn Hall
Interior design: Ragont Design
Cover design: Barb Fisher, LeVan Fisher Design
Cover photo and illustrations: © Swell Media/UpperCut/Getty Images and
                              Chen Ping Hung/Shutterstock
Author photo: Jeremy Sharp photography

Library of Congress Cataloging-in-Publication Data

Bunting, Karia Banks.
    Daddy's delight : embracing your divine design / Karia Banks Bunting.
      p. cm.
    Includes bibliographical references (p.   ).
    ISBN 978-0-8024-3688-7
    1. Christian women—Religious life. I. Title.
BV4527.B854 2010
248.8'43—dc22
                                                              2010001722

13 5 7 9 10 8 6 4 2

Printed in the United States of America.

*T*his book is dedicated to my father, Rev. Dr. Vernon M. Banks, who is now in heaven, enjoying himself. Thank you for spending countless hours praying for me, investing in me, explaining the Word to me, and demonstrating Christ. I remember the sparkle in your eye and your crooked smile as we engaged in theological discussions. I followed you as you followed Christ. I love you.

A special thanks to my pastor, Dr. Anthony Evans, and his wife, Dr. Lois Evans. I appreciate your investment in this servant of Christ. Thank you so much for your support and for allowing me to serve the Lord in your presence. I appreciate you.

Thank you to my family of sisters, the Life on Life Bible Study Group, at Oak Cliff. You know that I love you.

Contents

Foreword   9
Preface   11
Acknowledgments   15

Chapter 1
Your Divine Design   17

Chapter 2
Three Times a Lady   29

Chapter 3
Beauty and the Beast: Beating Satan at His Game   53

Chapter 4
Single and Significant   67

Chapter 5
Till Death Do You Part: Living Happy and Married   99

Chapter 6
Rocking Your World: The Blessing of Motherhood   131

Chapter 7
What to Do in the Midst of a Dilemma   157

Chapter 8
Finally Friends: The Importance of Relationships   167

Chapter 9
Minding Your Business: The Career of a Biblical Woman   183

Chapter 10
Called Out! When You Are Called into Ministry   209

Notes   227

Foreword

*I*t has been my joy and privilege to partner with my husband, Tony Evans, in the founding and development of our church in Dallas, called Oak Cliff Bible Fellowship. One of my ministries among many has been to oversee our women's fellowship. This is where we seek to inspire, equip, and encourage the women of God in their walk with the Lord.

One of our premier ministries in the women's fellowship is our Tuesday morning Life on Life Bible study. Ladies gather to hear the meaning and application of biblical truth taught by one of my core team leaders, Dr. Karia Bunting. Karia has been equipped and gifted by God to communicate God's Word in such a way that it both informs the mind while simultaneously touching the heart. Each week Karia challenges our women to know who they are in Christ, and see that reality express itself in the different dimensions of their lives.

God has uniquely prepared Karia for her life's calling—teaching women His truth. Armed with a doctorate in theology, coupled with the practical experience of raising a family, teaching at a university, and serving in the local church, Karia represents a unique sharp tool in the Master's hand.

In her first book, *Daddy's Delight*, Karia enables women to understand and experience their divine DNA. You will enjoy discovering who you are as the Creator sees you and how to live in light of this truth. *Daddy's Delight* will awaken you to the world of potential that is yours as you embrace your divine design. By the time you finish reading this engaging book, you will know exactly how to think and feel about yourself, based on how God has made you and how He wants to use you.

Daddy's Delight will enable every woman to realize how truly special you are as one of His daughters. It will also give you the tools to go further and deeper in your relationship with Him, yourself, and others. Every reader will discover afresh that you truly are fearfully and wonderfully made.

> For such a time as this,
> Lois Evans
> First Lady of Oak Cliff Bible Fellowship
> Senior Vice President of The Urban Alternative

Preface

Several years ago, as I attended a retreat, a young woman raised her hand and asked, "What does a godly woman look like?" I thought, *What a great question!* My own interpretation of what she really wanted to know is: what exactly is God's blueprint for us? What is our divine design?

When you examine your life, it is easy to focus on what you can readily see and recall. As your mind wanders, you notice the pretty fixtures of your finer features as well as the leaky faucets of your less-than-desirable ones. You enjoy the marble countertops of the habits you recently remodeled. It was hard work, but they are now polished and pretty.

You present with pride the fancy cabinetry of your culinary skills and the fruit of your good works. With concern and a little sadness, you observe the worn pattern on the carpets of your life where you've been trampled over and over again. You hide the red dye on the floor of the living room where somebody spilled something on you, covering the stain very carefully with a beautiful rug kept firmly in place by an expensive coffee table.

You wander around the private rooms of your life and are reminded of the crayon marks of happiness left by children or grandchildren, nieces or nephews, or your friend's two-year-old. Sometimes you note the chipped paint of unresolved issues that need repair and the holes where pictures of old relationships used to hang. Occasionally you pause to caress precious memorabilia from memories of love and the loss of days gone by.

Suddenly, you are jolted back to reality. Shaking your head, you spring into gear and turn your attention to whatever comes to your mind next: *I need to lose a few pounds. I've got to stop yelling at the kids. I must make sure dinner is ready when my husband gets home. We just bought a new house; I have to make more money. How do I make that happen? I have that meeting tonight. Honey, can you pick up the kids? There's a party this weekend, and I need to go to my nephew's game, but when am I going to fit all that in?*

My unmarried sisters might think, *I want to go to the singles' retreat next weekend, but I've got work and school. My hormones are raging . . . and I'm lonely.*

With so many thoughts swirling, you ask in desperation, "What now, Lord?" Then with one final attempt to pull yourself together, you give voice to your thoughts, "My quiet time is too noisy . . . and where in the world is my devotional book? Somebody moved it!"

Whether you are married, divorced, unmarried, or a widow and your desire is to be a godly woman—you probably find yourself rowing against the current of today's culture. It's hard to hold your ground with so many temptations lurking around every bend in life.

Perhaps you are a stay-at-home mom and absolutely delight in your job. Still there are those days when you identify with the brilliant poet Langston Hughes: "What happens to a dream deferred? Does it dry up, like a raisin in the sun?"[1] Then on other days when you're tutoring the kids you find yourself identifying with the character "Count von Count" from *Sesame Street:* "One . . . one cookie on the floor. Two . . . two cookies on the floor. Three . . . "

The pressure on you seems increasingly intense. It makes you scream with internal frustration when you think about that "one more thing" you have to do. All too often it appears as if you will never accomplish your goals. Every now and then tears begin to flow down your cheeks: when your husband is especially insensitive, your friends are unavailable for consolation, there are unreasonable expectations at the office, your bills are due and you don't have the money, your neighbors are pestering you to cut your tree back, a storm blows over your fence, or your youngest child gets a series of red check marks in her homework folder.

Sometimes you're happy and excited, but at other times you're tired and confused. Nevertheless, you have a heart for God. In the midst of all this, while you're trying hard to keep it together, you can't help but wonder: *What does a godly woman look like?*

Could it be possible that the difficulty you have in coping with life's issues lies in the fact that your concern is only with the external things you can see? May I suggest to you that having an inward focus and considering how you are internally made will yield more effective results? Maybe your "picture" of yourself is falling off the wall because it was not God's idea for you in the first place.

Maybe the reason that there is a crack in the ceiling of your life is because there is a crack in the foundation of your life. And just maybe you are trying to become the virtuous woman of Proverbs 31, not realizing that this wonderful description gives you the goal but not the guidance to achieve it. It provides the destination without the road map, the car, or the driver's manual.

But in the midst of your musing, here is something for you to ponder. When Jesus said in Matthew 11:30: *"For My yoke is easy and My burden is light,"* what on earth does that mean to a woman?

Read this book to discover answers to some of the pertinent issues that you struggle with daily. It will give you the tools that you need to maximize your existence as a woman after God's heart. Dear sister, no matter in what category of womanhood you find yourself, you will learn how our heavenly Father meticulously designed you. You will also discover how to apply His design to your life day by day. Then as you embrace His plan for your success, you will find yourself more at peace; and therefore—less stressed out. Learn how to be better at being who you are. Enjoy your identity and divine provision. You are "Daddy's delight".

I love stationery. I even drag my husband into stationery stores to browse through the various paraphernalia with me. Recently, we were grabbing some Chinese food when I spotted a stationery store two doors down. I quickly placed my takeout order and dashed back to my husband who was waiting in the car. "Come and go into the stationery store with me!" I exclaimed. He looked at me with "those" eyes and simply obliged my request. We walked around and looked at the exciting party invitations and elegant wedding invitations (I still have two unmarried daughters). Then we made our way over to the seemingly endless array of notepads, greeting cards, and so on.

There was one notepad in particular that caught my eye and brought a smile to my face. I picked it up and took it over to my husband. He read the inscription at the bottom of the pad and asked, "What does that mean?" The inscription read: "If the crown fits . . ." I explained that every time I picked up the pad to write a note on it, I would have to read that quote. And every time I read it, I would be reminded of something. It would be a moment of *rhema* for me—and I would gain a deeper understanding of who I am. I am a child of the King of kings. I am divinely designed. I am significant to God. What I say and do matters. I have been gifted, equipped, and sent to do God's will.

In other words, that notepad would inspire me and motivate me to do what I was designed to do—and be who God designed me to be. When I wrote something on it, I would be prompted to read the bottom line, printed boldly in beautiful script: *"If the crown fits . . ."* Then I would be compelled to complete the phrase: "wear it."[2]

I want to wear my crown. I want to show off my inheritance. I want to demonstrate my royalty. That is my desire, but what about you? Think of this book as my note to you, written on a notepad. On the bottom of the page God has written you a subtext that reads: "My daughter, since the crown fits . . ."

From this day forward, since the crown fits, God wants you to wear it! Be the woman whom God created you to be. Understand how marvelously you were fashioned by God, and experience the joy of being divinely designed.

Acknowledgments

To My Family,

   Thank you for your love and support. Thank you, Tristin, for your dedication to the ministry and for the hours you invested in this work. May God give you the desires of your heart. Thank you, Ryan and Kimberly, for being Mom's cheerleaders. You are my heart. You are always there to offer words of encouragement. And you are so much fun to hang out with when I am not working. I am proud of you.

   Most of all, thank you, George. You supported me for seventeen years while I studied the Word of God. Thank you for your love and your commitment. Thank you for sacrificing so that God could talk to His people through us. You are my partner and my friend. I will always love you.

—Karia

Your Divine Design

GOD'S PICASSO

Have you ever seen something so beautiful that it almost takes your breath away? Last year my family went to Africa. After de-boarding the plane, we rode in Jeeps to the compound where we would be staying. The heart of the people reached out to greet us as we drove down the narrow pathway toward the inland. I had never before seen greener trees, denser forests, redder dirt, or clearer streams. The countryside exuded exquisite beauty. If you had been sitting next to me on that bumpy, safari-like ride, every few minutes you could have heard me quietly exhale, "Oh, my goodness," as I observed the untouched beauty of God's creative finger. In fashioning the continent of Africa, God has truly created a masterpiece.

As I continued to contemplate God's creative genius, I turned my attention to His greatest creation—human beings. I couldn't help but wonder at the marvelous design with which He made us. You and I reflect the beautiful labor of God's love. When I look at my life, I see the hand of God's intricate blueprint at work. He has gifted every one of us in an exceptional way that enables us to excel in our own creativity.

By now you have probably discovered a certain talent that sets you apart from the rest; others recognize your God-given gift as well. If you enjoy cooking, perhaps your kitchen embodies the cradle of creativity. Nobody can beat your fried apples, chicken salad, crab cakes, homemade rolls, greens, or sweet potato pie. The sensual scent of your delightful delicacies mesmerizes anyone blessed to drop by for a visit. When you place that much-anticipated final touch on your special meal, you whisper, "Ah . . . that's good." Your table has become a culinary masterpiece.

Yes, every one of us has been graciously blessed by our Creator. Knowing this should give us pause to reflect on God's excellent design and marvel at His goodness. Scripture proclaims to us who we are, "*We are His workmanship, created in Christ Jesus for good works, which God prepared beforehand so that we would walk in them*" (Ephesians 2:10). The Greek word "workmanship" has the same root as the English word "poem." It refers to a creation of some sort, a work of art; a masterstroke of brilliance.

In the mind of God, you are a creation far greater than Leonardo da Vinci's striking portrait *Mona Lisa* or Maya Angelou's insightful poem *Phenomenal Woman*. You are a masterwork more lovely than the Eiffel Tower of Paris and Rotterdam's Swan Bridge. You are more stunning than the Alps of Switzerland and stronger than the glaciers of the Antarctic. When the wind adorns your hair, the majestic plains of Africa pale in comparison to your beauty. The Grand Canyon lacks the depth to search your soul. You are a crowning creation; you are God's Picasso. When God made you, He created a masterpiece and declared, "Ah, that's good."

YOUR NAME IS VICTORY

For a number of reasons, maybe you don't feel like a work of art on this particular day. In your opinion you're either too skinny or too fat. You may have PMS symptoms that are causing you to be bloated and grouchy. At this moment you might just feel like pulling off every piece of clothing you're wearing because you are having the biggest hot flash this side of heaven! Maybe you are in your ninth month of pregnancy, feeling like an overinflated balloon with nowhere to turn for comfort. Nevertheless, in whatever way you describe yourself, in God's eyes you still reflect His greatest creation.

As a single person, did you ever have to endure the experience of someone else's wedding celebration at a time when you were longing for a mate? You probably sat there with a smile on your face while silently your heart was aching. In situations like that, it's easy to feel like you are nothing special. But you are. Maybe your husband or boyfriend cheated on you and now you are wondering why you weren't good enough. You were. Maybe that costly mistake you made makes you feel worthless. You are still a masterpiece. Maybe you were abused and nobody else knows about it. You think, *If I am such a masterpiece, how could that have happened? I might be a torn work of art, but never the real thing.* Know that you are precious to God. He delights in you. You are His work of genius.

Whatever your state of mind may be, God wants to have an intimate relationship with you. He wants to bless you, redeem you, and heal you. In fact, your heavenly Father has planned a lifetime of good things for you to do. To make sure that you accomplish them, He will orchestrate the events of your life so that you will use everything you have experienced for His glory. For this reason, it is important that you recognize how valuable you are to God. He wants you to listen to what He is saying to you through your daily trials. Reach out to Him for answers that will transform and improve your life. He is reaching out to you.

But you say, "What about how I feel?" You must understand that your feelings are not reliable and they don't always reflect the truth. Only the Word of God is truth—it is dependable and trustworthy—and it never changes. Have you ever felt one way about something and, after you got more information, you reacted in a completely different way? A shift in circumstances can cause a change in your perception about a given situation. Even though you can't always depend on them, the Lord understands that your emotions can sometimes get the best of you. Scripture even tells us that Jesus is touched by our feelings: *"For we do not have a high priest who cannot sympathize with our weaknesses, but One who has been tempted in all things as we are, yet without sin"* (Hebrews 4:15).

Jesus knows how you feel because He shared those same feelings. But, as the Son of God, He has the power to help you defeat everything that hinders you from moving forward. He wants you to move past your emotions and rely on Him so that you can see your circumstances in a different light—the light of His loving concern. It's not about the way that you feel about a problem; it's your faith in Jesus' power that will conquer every challenge. Faith will allow you to depend on His strength to overcome those stubborn feelings that would keep you stuck in the past. Jesus wants you to live a victorious life. Always have these words on your lips and remember to say of our Lord, *"I can do all things through Him who strengthens me"* (Philippians 4:13).

The truth of the matter is, even when you feel like God doesn't love you, He does. His love is a fact. His love for you is true—regardless of what you are going through. Love Him back. He'll show you who He is and how much He really does care. Even during the times when you might want to quit because you feel like you are too far behind, finish the race. You will win.

You will be able to echo the words to Jonathan Nelson's song "My Name is Victory":[3]

> I've got evidence
> I've got confidence
> I'm a conqueror
> I know that I win
> I know who I am
> God wrote it in His plan for me
> MY NAME IS VICTORY!

As a believer in Christ, victory belongs to you. The good works you are going to perform are already ordained for you. Breathe in and step out. Do what God tells you to do and He will do the rest. Remember, your name is "Victory."

GOD'S SPITTING IMAGE

My youngest daughter, Kimberly, looks just like her father. She has his eyes and, definitely, his nose. She also has a big smile and a petite face. If you were to look at her and then at him, you would know that she is his daughter. Here in Texas they would say, "He spit 'er out, didn't he?" She is the spitting image of her daddy.

In a comparable way, God created His children to look like Him. When the conversation ensued in the boardroom of heaven, God the Father was talking to Jesus and the Holy Spirit. He said, *"Let Us make man in Our image, according to Our likeness; and let them rule over the fish of the sea and over the birds of the sky and over the cattle and over all the earth, and over every creeping thing that creeps on the earth"* (Genesis 1:26). This Scripture gives us insight into how we resemble our Creator. Similar to the way in which He rules heaven, God gave His offspring the ability to rule the earth.

When God the Father, God the Son, and God the Holy Spirit agreed to the plan, God created Adam from the dust of the ground (Genesis 2:7). This is an important distinction to understand. Human flesh is different from the flesh of animals. Scripture reveals this truth in 1 Corinthians 15:39, as it describes the makeup of God's creatures, *"All flesh is not the same flesh, but there is one flesh of men, and another flesh of beasts, and another flesh of birds, and another of fish."* From this verse we are assured that neither you nor I evolved from an ape. We are not human animals. We are different from all other living beings. We are created by God, for God. In urban street jargon, every one of us is God's "Mini-Me."

Listen to how I envision God creating woman. Eve waited silently in Adam's side. Suddenly, God caused her covering to slumber. When

His firm tug removed her from her waiting place, God had a magnificent design in mind. He carefully built her, lovingly forming her gentle shape.

The wedding was beautiful. Officiated and witnessed by the Trinity of God, the question was put forth, "Who gives this woman to be lawfully wedded to this man?" The response, "I do." Then God presented Eve to her husband. Adam's vows echoed throughout the Garden: *"This is now bone of my bones, and flesh of my flesh"* (Genesis 2:23). God stepped back. She was Adam's woman.

In all of its magnificent array, the Garden was perfect. It was time for the Father's toast. What would God's blessing be? God proudly smiled at His newlyweds and commanded them to, *"Be fruitful and multiply, and fill the earth, and subdue it"* (Genesis 1:28).

Just like Eve, at some point in time we all find ourselves in our waiting place. The message from heaven to every woman is: wait on. At the proper time, when your environment is ready and you have completed your development, you will feel God's firm tug move you to a different place. You will find yourself established in your appointed purpose.

A GROUND FLOOR OPPORTUNITY

New organizations often offer ground floor opportunities. This means when individuals join a company at its beginning, their work helps to set the stage for what the company eventually becomes. Every employee has an integral part to play because the outcome of the business is relying on the contributions of the workers. If they are successful, the company is successful. However, if they fail to contribute positively, the company fails.

Adam and Eve had a ground floor opportunity. In His powerful words of blessing, God gave them the authority to conquer the world. They were groomed for success. They could reproduce God's image and expand their control through numbers. As such, the future of humanity was in their hands.

You might say, "That was Adam and Eve, but what about me?" Well, I have good news for you. God has not rescinded His decree. The power and authority God gave to Adam and Eve is passed on to you and me. With the power you have been delegated, you have the authority to be fruitful and multiply. Fill the earth with as many children as God gives you (either biologically or spiritually) and subdue your world. In essence, you have a ground floor opportunity to make of your life whatever God planned for you.

Your good works are waiting for you. You can dominate what you see within your sphere of influence. And when you doubt yourself, remember these reassuring words: if God is for you, no one can effectively be against you. You are equipped to be victorious. You have been blessed to succeed. God has made Himself available to you so that you can ultimately reign triumphant.

So the question then becomes: what more do you need? You may say, "I need more money." But when God blessed Adam and Eve, they had no money. They had the covering of God's Word—and His Word is faithful and true. That's all they needed. God's Word in your life is all that you need. It is alive, and it will accomplish what God sent it to do. If God says do something, do it. You don't have to fear or feel inadequate. He will make it happen. He will even straighten out your mess. He is sufficient for you.

You might also say, "I need more time." You have the same amount of time in a day that Adam and Eve had. If you say, "I can't," God says you can. When you say, "I'm tired," God has energy for you. If you happen to say, "I'm weary. Life has been hard," God would say, "Yes, but it is not over." That means there is something left for you to do. Instead of relying on your abilities, the more productive thing to do is develop an exclusive dependence on God's powerful Word to sustain you. He will renew and direct you. You can do it because God wants you to do it. No more excuses. It's time to subdue your world.

A BABE IN THE WOODS

One day when I needed to make a call, my cell phone wasn't handy. So I picked up my husband's phone instead. When I looked at the screen, it had recorded a missed call from someone named "A Babe." My brow furrowed. "Who is this, George?" I asked. He smiled wickedly. "A Babe," he responded. "What Babe?" I asked. He proceeded to make up this wild story about some woman who insisted that he put her number in his phone.

By now, the children had gathered to listen. You have to understand, I am the ultimate believer. If he says something, I believe it. So I was standing there, looking at him with a perplexed expression on my face, as if to say, "What???" Finally, he couldn't hold it in any longer. He bent over laughing, and the kids did too. Apparently, I was the only one who didn't get the joke. "What are you laughing about?" I asked. "Karia, that's your number. You are "A Babe," he explained. "Oh," I responded. "Okay." They couldn't stop laughing. Evidently the kids knew already. The joke was on me! I'm glad he still thinks of me as "a babe" after twenty-six years!

Eve was "a babe" in the woods. She was in a pleasant environment and couldn't have asked for anything more. God set her up. She had a beautiful home—the Garden of Eden—no less. She had a wonderful husband who loved her. She had a bright future. But she also had a dark side; she didn't really trust God. She questioned His heart and His Word. Her trust issue soon turned into disobedience. Unfortunately, that disobedience would become the demise of her world as she knew it.

Throughout the Garden, there were animals everywhere. One of them talked to her. It was Satan preying on her in the form of a serpent, but Eve didn't recognize him as a threat. I wonder how he sounded. Was his voice gentle and smooth, or rough and harsh? Was it sweet like ice cream, or deep and sinister? Did he imitate God's voice when he spoke? More than likely, he sounded like whatever would be most enticing to Eve.

Some of us have Eve's problem; we don't fully trust what God is saying to us. We know that He has clearly spoken to us about something that will greatly affect our lives, but the choice is ours to make between God's provision and protection and Satan's deadly trap. If we choose to follow the wrong voice, we immediately become susceptible to harm. Please heed this word of caution. Having a lack of trust in God can put you in a dangerous situation, because it means that you are vulnerable to temptation from the enemy. He is ever ready to entice you away from the place of God's shelter and blessings. And when we don't obey God's voice, we put ourselves in a position to get seriously hurt.

How does Satan sound when he whispers in your ear? Does he sound like your boyfriend? Like a father figure? Like a trusted leader? You can avoid Eve's mistake by spending time with God and reading His Word. This is the process by which you build up your faith and trust in Him. You will learn to recognize when Satan is speaking and discern the difference between his deceptive prompts and God's voice of inspiration.

Jesus boldly proclaimed in John 10:27, *"My sheep hear My voice, and I know them, and they follow Me."* His words assure us that we have the ability to recognize His voice. Follow it with confidence. When you keep His Word deep in your heart, you won't have to doubt when God is speaking.

YOUR WONDERFUL PRESENT

Christmas is an amazing time in the Bunting household. Our family delights in such exciting time-honored traditions as our ceremonial tree topping. On Christmas Eve, amidst great fanfare, clapping, and hooting, one of our gleeful children gingerly climbs the shaky ladder. That fortunate child finally arrives at the crown of the tallest evergreen that could be found at the last minute under the cold outdoor tree sales tent.

After firmly placing the lighted star atop the single stalk pointing heavenward, he or she slowly descends to the accolades of relatives cheering and calling out his or her name. Finally reaching the bottom rung, the happy sibling slowly surrenders the coveted spot to another as the debate arises about whose turn it will be next year.

Early the next morning of that glorious day, baked red apples stuffed with cinnamon are passed around on cherished Christmas plates—one per person. The family then gathers to enjoy a passionate Bible study led by my husband. Next comes the singing of nativity songs while bacon sizzles in the oven and bread rises on the countertop.

Soon leaves will be added to the dining room table where the family and friends who drop by for dinner will enjoy a nicely browned turkey, cornbread dressing, glazed ham, and the celebrated broccoli and cheese casserole that is served only on Easter, Thanksgiving, and Christmas. A cornucopia of vegetables, salads, pies, and cakes also contribute their sumptuous delights.

Once devotions and Bible study are complete, the feature of the much-anticipated day is the interminable opening of gifts. On a rotating basis, each person opens one gift at a time. "Who's that from? That's from me!" Comments such as these can be heard as members of the family delightedly tear through the bright wrapping paper to see what gift offering from the heart awaits them.

Truly it is a blessed day from beginning to end. However, it doesn't compare to the fun and festivities God has planned for our future. He has given us all the most precious present He has to offer—His heart. If you respond from your heart by loving Him, seeking Him, and worshiping Him, He slowly unwraps Himself for you. Your hearts connect. Suddenly, you find yourself in meadows of peace, tiptoeing through flowers of joy. As you savor the pleasure of His divine company, all will be well with your soul. You can rest assured that no matter what is going on around you, you are protected by your heavenly Daddy.

My sentiments reflect the abundance of God's best for you. Every morning, His loving-kindness wakes you up. He whispers, "I love you" and you quickly respond, "I love you, too, Daddy." The Spirit of God then reminds you, "I'm going to take care of you today. Don't worry about anything." You smile and say, "Okay, Dad. I won't." Then He says, "Now, go get 'em, girl!"

Before you arise from your bed, God has already equipped you with grace and mercy. You have a new day and a new chance to be all He has called you to be. He holds nothing against you once you admit your wrongs. If you need anything, He's right there. If you are hurt, He becomes your Healer. Your heavenly Father thinks about you day and night. He loves you so much.

King David recognized the significance of God's love. He recalls, *"When I consider Your heavens, the work of Your fingers, the moon and the stars, which You have ordained; what is man that You take thought of him, and the son of man that You care for him? Yet You have made him a little lower than God, and You crown him with glory and majesty"* (Psalm 8:3–5). Right now, my sister, God is thinking about you. He gives you Himself. In Him you have all you need. Each and every day you can walk in the truth and knowledge that you are God's delight.

Three Times a Lady

HOW TO ENJOY BEING A WOMAN

Raquel is always laughing. When she enters the church, she greets everyone with a warm hug and a word of encouragement. Her compassion sparkles through her eyes. She guides her children toward their seats as she carries herself with poise and exuberance. Raquel's personality makes people sit up and take notice of her; they gaze at her with an approving smile.

Sister Janice's appearance is always tidy and neat; her pin curls never seem to move. Her hat carefully pinned and her Bible and handkerchief in hand, she makes her way into church early on Sunday mornings. Before the general Sunday school session begins, she is lovingly greeted by the younger ladies. "How are you, sister?" She answers, "Jus' fine, 'n you?" Their warm responses trail behind her flowery dress, "Fine, thank you." She continues on to take her seat. "Thas' good. Thas' good."

After service, Janice labors to open the creaking back door and slowly descends the steep steps. Happily she makes her way home to prepare her peach cobbler in time for dinner. Sister Janice is a wise and dedicated woman of God who, over her long life, has gained a lifetime of wisdom and experiences.

Kimberly's character defines a woman of excellence. Dignified and affectionate, her presence manifests a gentle grace. She commands attention without trying and attracts admiring glances from bystanders. Confidently walking toward the front of the beautiful sanctuary, she seats herself on the front pew. Dressed in a linen suit, hair perfectly coiffed and lips gently glazed in the softest pink, she smiles warmly as fellow ladies of the church join her for worship. The soft tone of her voice and the sparkle of her bright smile offer pleasant comfort for everyone whom she encounters.

From the examples of the women described above, one could conclude that they all seem to be secure in their personalities and with who God made them. God has created every woman with her own unique characteristics. He has given us strengths and abilities that allow us to grow and develop according to the purpose He has deemed for each individual. Yet living a godly life does not depend on one's personality. It depends on the freedom of choice we have to take the path that He has set before us—the path of righteousness and truth.

God wants you to have the determination to be who He made you to be. He expects you to pursue the divine purpose that He has given you. The Son has set you free to be you. He is pleased when you enjoy your life as you grow and develop into being a godly woman.

To know your true self, you must give God access to all of you. Allow Him entrance into your deepest, most intimate thoughts. As you do so, He will work with you to clean up your struggles and challenges and help you overcome the thoughts and behaviors that are holding you back. Every step that you take in cooperation with God reveals more of who you are in Him. You will come closer and closer to mirroring the design of a godly woman and becoming the individual that God has determined you to be.

For example, if you have interpersonal relationships that are messy and difficult to manage, the first person to look at is yourself and what you need to do differently. When you ask Him to show you, God will shine the light of the Holy Spirit on your flaws so you can correct your faulty behaviors. And by the grace that He gives you, the change will begin to take place.

You should know that there is a process involved and it won't happen overnight. So don't be discouraged. Rather, be encouraged by the positive results that will also become evident. At the same time that God's light is shining on your weaknesses, your potential to reflect His ultimate design for you will also come to the light. You will begin to see who He called you to be.

Moreover, when you invite the Holy Spirit to teach you how to manage your finances, He will help you to be more prosperous so that you can increase your ability to do good things with your money. You will discover which of your financial habits are productive, and which ones aren't. Allow the principles of God's Word to influence your money; study them and let them inform your decisions about what to do with the funds that you generate. You will realize your financial potential—and learn how to pursue it wisely.

Your time is extremely important. There is only so much that you can accomplish in twenty-four hours. When you give God access to your daily habits, He will help you organize your schedule. The more that you seek to please Him on a daily basis, He will make your productivity that much greater. You will become satisfied and content with the way in which you manage your time.

Now take a good look inside your closet. Are you satisfied with what you see? The way in which you dress reflects your self-respect. A godly woman is both modest and stylish in her attire. But she also understands that clothing does not make a woman. The wisdom that we receive from the Word of God warns against the tendency to be fixated on physical adornments. Listen to what the apostle Peter taught the women in the church of his day, "*Your adornment must not be merely external—braiding the hair, and wearing gold jewelry, or putting*

on dresses; but let it be the hidden person of the heart, with the imperish-
able quality of a gentle and quiet spirit, which is precious in the sight of
God" (1 Peter 3:3–4). Wise women understand that it is not the out-
ward appearance that is most important; rather, it is the content of the
heart that pleases Him.

Finally, when God has access to your heart, the Holy Spirit will
teach you how to love Him by loving others. He will also help you
appreciate yourself even more. Stand before the mirror of His Word
and see how to shape the image of your divine design according to
God's likeness.

God wants you to be a well-rounded woman who pursues His will
and acts in obedience to Him. However, to be a woman of God, you
have to first enjoy being a woman. Part of a woman's spiritual DNA
is to want the most out of life and to get enjoyment and fulfillment
out of doing the things God has designed us to do. Playing sports is one
way to find satisfaction. Women who are physically active enjoy such
sports as: golfing, swimming, basketball, tennis, volleyball, and base-
ball. These activities provide good exercise to help maintain proper
health.

Mental fitness is another key factor in staying healthy; therefore,
exercising the mind by being well-read is very important. Yet the most
significant thing about being a woman has to do with utilizing the gifts
God gave us. We have been given the ability to contribute to society
in countless ways, including as: politicians, educators, students, cooks,
gardeners, nurses, doctors, and engineers.

When I graduated from college in the early 1980s (okay, I'm dating
myself), the female students majoring in business were taught to take
on masculine characteristics in the workplace. To achieve maximum
success, we were expected to wear stiff blue suits, conservative hair-
styles, a minimum of makeup, and no perfume. We were taught to
stand like a man, jockey for positions in the boardroom like a man, and
be aggressive and competitive. To maintain the appropriate posture in
negotiating and decision making, we learned to effectively use stern,
serious voices and not to smile.

Although contrary to the softer feminine side of our nature, that type of behavior garnered prominent jobs with high-paying salaries. But a problem surfaced when we got married and started our families. The duties of motherhood demanded workplace changes to accommodate our new responsibilities. It became our job to care for our infants and toddlers and then make the transition to day care. We also needed to take sick days and vacation time to work around childhood illnesses and school schedules.

Overall, career women required a sufficient work/life balance. We insisted on mommy tracks, family leave for both genders, and forced the trend toward working from home. This all happened when we became who we were destined to be in the workplace—career women with the responsibilities of having a family. This description may or may not define you. As a wife and mother, you may have a different work experience and lifestyle. My point is, be who you are. Become the best woman you can be and fulfill your responsibilities according to the design of your life.

Whatever your personal circumstances may demand of you, nobody can be you as well as you. God gave everyone of us a unique design and we are most successful when we embrace that design. There is no reason to feel less important than anyone else. Being yourself will work to your advantage. Take delight in your divine design.

THE MANNER OF A GODLY WOMAN

The definition of a godly woman means that your character matches God's character. Isn't it funny how, when two people spend a lot of time together, they begin to display similar characteristics? When you spend a lot of time with Jesus, you take on His mind-set and begin to act like Him. The best way to spend time with Jesus is by studying His life and applying God's Word to your life. As you get to know Jesus' character better, the Holy Spirit will transform you so that you begin to think and talk in ways that follow Jesus' example.

The more that you imitate His ways, the more your manner will reflect the fruit of the Spirit found in Galatians 5:22: love, joy, peace, patience, kindness, goodness, faithfulness, gentleness, and self-control. These are the godly qualities that mirror the image of God in your personality.

Love

There is a very familiar song by musical artist Tina Turner that asked the question, "What's Love Got to Do with It?" Some of the words of the song are, *What's love got to do with it? Who needs a heart when a heart can be broken?*[4]

These two questions are very relevant to life. It is quite a paradox to me that the very people whom you love are the ones who can hurt you the most. Because your heart is vulnerable to them, you are susceptible to heartbreak brought about by loved ones. God the Father loved the first two human beings that He created, but Adam and Eve broke His heart. Jesus loved mankind enough to give His life for us, and humanity broke His heart.

If you have loved and been hurt, this is a time to change your focus and make God the focal point of your love and attention. More than you need another person's love, you need to know the love of God. He will help you get over the pain and help you to recover from a broken heart. The truth is that you need to be involved with someone who loves you back. And there is only one person who does that perfectly—and that is Jesus.

Our Lord and Savior loves you unconditionally, and He will never break your heart. He expressed the depth of His love when He proclaimed that, *"Greater love has no one than this, that one lay down his life for his friends"* (John 15:13). Jesus is your best Friend. He loved you enough to die for you before you were even born. His powerful love can heal your broken heart.

You will begin to heal when you focus on the love that Jesus provides. Listen to the guidance that He gives through His Word. Scripture says in Hebrews 12:2 that Jesus is the author and finisher of your faith. He can bring you through difficult issues in life. He has already prepared the way for you to overcome your pain. You only need to put your faith in His supreme love and obey Him. If the wind, the sea, and spirits obey Him—you can too. Even if you are sick in your body, He hears your cry. If you could ask the sick woman who reached out for Him in Luke 8:48, she would testify that He is a Healer.

There are few greater joys in life than loving people. If you have the Spirit of God in you, the love of God must be suppressed in order for it not to show. Maybe there is something in your past that has affected your ability to give yourself completely and to love unconditionally. Let the Word of God help you renew your mind. As you study and apply the Scriptures related to God's love, your heart will turn to Him and reflect the love He has placed within you.

How does this work? Let's use a practical example. Marie works hard. She lives with her family but mostly keeps to herself. She loves a certain brand of cola and is not happy unless she has her favorite cola every day. Marie usually buys a week's supply of small bottles and stores them on the top shelf of the refrigerator. If anyone touches *her* drink, she is angry, rude, and disrespectful. One day while Marie was reading the Bible, she paused and read, "[love] *does not act unbecomingly; it does not seek its own, is not provoked, does not take into account a wrong suffered*" (1 Corinthians 13:4).

Without fully understanding why, she felt compelled to apply this principle in her life. The Word of God had penetrated her heart. Marie decided not only to stop getting angry if someone drank her cola, but that she would start buying larger bottles rather than the personal size bottles so that there would be enough to share.

Through her response to God's Word, she has intentionally shown love to the people in her family. In essence, Marie has changed her mind about how she would behave from now on. Feeling a good deal of satisfaction, Marie senses that God is pleased with her actions. She is motivated to continue her new practice and notices another habit that violates the Word of God. As she begins to meditate on Scriptures that apply to changing her behavior, she finds it easier to obey what she knows in her heart to be right.

Marie's mind is being transformed by the renewing of the Word, and the people around her benefit from her expression of God's love. Learn to love by transforming your mind with the Word of God.

Joy

A godly woman finds joy in her life. Even though her circumstances are not always great, she has a quiet confidence that everything is going to work out for good. She recognizes that a joyful attitude is a deep inner sense of gladness that does not depend on circumstances. As a result, her joy comes from trusting God.

Sometimes when we are learning to trust God, joy can become elusive. These are times when we need to find joy by relying on our greatest resource. When trouble comes and circumstances are beyond our control, we can call on Jesus. He sends the help we need to fix the mess. Call on Him with the assurance that He will answer. Even in the midst of difficulty, Jesus will give you the ability to be joyful.

In the book of 2 Kings, chapter 4, the story is told of a woman who had joy in the midst of a problem. This woman was a business owner who was well-known throughout her community. The prophet Elisha would visit her city quite frequently. Whenever he visited, she would invite him to her home for dinner. One day she had an idea. She decided to remodel the space upstairs and make a room for him. That way he could stay with her family whenever he came to town. Her husband agreed, and they built Elisha a beautiful bedroom, very nicely furnished.

One day Elisha was resting in his room and was inspired to do something for her. He summoned her and said, *"At this season next year you will embrace a son"* (2 Kings 4:16a). Her unspoken desire for a child had been so deep that his words initially hurt her. It caused her to exclaim, *"No, my lord, O man of God, do not lie to your maidservant"* (2 Kings 4:16b).

But the next year she did have a son. However, the boy would not live many years before something terrible happened. One day he was out in the field with his father. When he came down with a headache, the servants brought him inside. Within hours, he died in his mother's lap. She laid the boy on Elisha's bed, got a donkey, and told her husband she was going to get the man of God. He asked her what was going on, and she told him that everything was fine.

Ladies, that's real joy. If you can say that everything is fine when your life is falling apart, you are trusting God to put it back together. The woman went to find Elisha. When he saw her coming, he anxiously sent his servant to ask her if everything was well with her, her husband, and her child. She told the servant too that everything was fine. But when she got to the man of God, she let it all go. She fell at his feet and insisted that he come and help. He did. Elisha lay on the child and by the power of the Most High brought the boy back to life (see 2 Kings 4:32–37).

When your circumstances are dead, nobody can help you—but Jesus. You can truly say that everything is fine because you know it is just a matter of time until God resuscitates your dead situation. Wait on Him to show up—you won't be disappointed. While you are waiting, show God your faith and watch Him redeem what others may think is unredeemable in your life. In the interim, as you continue to trust Him for the answer, your confidence in Him will be the source of your joy.

Jesus told His disciples, *"Until now you have asked for nothing in My name; ask and you will receive, so that your joy may be made full"* (John 16:24). Our Lord wants you to have joy. He is inviting you to ask Him for what you need so that He can give you cause to rejoice.

Peace

A few years ago, I noticed young people greeting each other with the two-finger victory sign turned toward the left. As they made this gesture, they would exclaim, "Peace!" When departing, they would do the same thing, saying, "Peace out!" I thought that was so cool! It was an expression of peace toward others. During biblical times, people greeted each other with the word "shalom," which also means "peace."

Amidst so many atrocities and hardship in the world, no wonder peace is so important! The word "peace" means freedom from disquiet or oppressive thoughts. Peace, then, is a state of tranquility; it is inherently the absence of rage and havoc. In your heart, is there peace or a raging battle? It is difficult to demonstrate love or joy when you have no peace. If there is a fight going on inside of you, it will show up on the outside.

Where does peace originate? How do we access it? Christ says in John 14:27, *"Peace I leave with you; My peace I give to you; not as the world gives do I give to you. Do not let your heart be troubled, nor let it be fearful."* Peace is a gift from Christ. It belongs to Him, and He gives it to you and me. The reason you cannot have peace without Christ is that you must find it in Him. He gives it to those who trust Him. Scripture tells us that His peace keeps you from doing two things: (1) having a troubled heart and (2) being afraid.

Jesus said, *"Do not let your heart be troubled."* It is a command from God. This means that you have control over whether your heart is troubled, because God gives us the ability to follow His commands. You can tell the difference between a troubled heart and one free from trouble: is your confidence in yourself or Christ? If your confidence is in yourself, you have plenty of reason for your heart to be troubled. Chaos could break out in your life at any time and there would be nothing you could do about it! You have decided to deal with it on your own.

On the other hand, if your confidence is in Christ, you can decide not to be troubled and Jesus will back you up. Scripture reminds us that *"the peace of God, which surpasses all comprehension, will guard your hearts and your minds in Christ Jesus"* (Philippians 4:7). He has given us His peace so that when challenges come we can face them without fear.

If you allow it to, fear can destroy your peace and debilitate your life. Sometimes it is subtle. There are many reasons why people feel afraid. Some people are afraid of failure or success. They may be afraid that things won't get better. They might be afraid to go to work because they fear getting fired. They are afraid when the telephone rings because it might be bad news. They are afraid to go out because someone could harm them. At the same time, they are afraid of staying at home for the same reason. Some people are afraid of a friend or mate because they have been hurt by them. Others are afraid to start a business because it could fail.

This is the second reason Jesus left us with His peace—so that we would not be fearful. Fear works against peace, and God wants us to know that we do not have to accept fear over peace. Scripture reminds us that *"God hath not given us the spirit of fear; but of power, and of love, and of a sound mind"* (2 Timothy 1:7 KJV). Fear is a spirit that God does not give. Your enemy, the devil, gives it to you. But it is something that you can reject. Many times in the Bible people were told to "take courage!" You can decide not to be afraid and choose to trust God—that is taking courage over fear.

My grandmother lived in a house by herself in a bad, drug-infested neighborhood until she was ninety-two. When I asked her if she was afraid, she said, "No!" One day someone came up to her back porch in the middle of the night. She woke up and heard them. She went into the kitchen, which was adjacent to her back porch, and yelled, "If you don't get off my back porch I am going to kill you!" They left! When she was in danger, she took courage from God and rejected fear from the enemy. She continued to live in her home and would not allow the neighborhood to intimidate her at all. When she finally had to leave because of illness, she was not happy about it!

Fear feeds on itself and causes stagnation in life. There's no wonder why we can't move forward. When we have accepted the spirit of fear, Satan doesn't need much more to defeat us. Ask yourself what you are afraid of and take it to the Lord. He has given you the power to reject the fear and replace it with His peace. When you choose not to be afraid, you have chosen to side with God and that dramatically changes your situation. Now you can overcome your fear through your faith in God.

Faith

Faith is believing in what God says. Faith is not a wish, a hope, or a dream. The Bible says that it is more solid than that. Listen to the

Word describe what faith is, *"Now faith is the assurance of things hoped for, the conviction of things not seen"* (Hebrews 11:1).

This is the way faith works: God has made promises through His Word. He may have spoken to your heart about one of His promises when you were studying the Bible or when the preacher was delivering his message. You know that God spoke to you. You believe what He said. You have put your trust in Him to do it. That's faith.

Now, because you believe what He said, you act on it. That is called works. The proof that God gave you a promise and you believe it will happen is what prompts you to action. You begin to do something and take steps toward achieving the thing that you desire. When you mix your faith together with works, you get what you hope for.

Let's make it practical. Let's say that you have come to believe that God is going to do a miracle in your life. He is going to give you something that your heart deeply wants. You've always wanted to be a special education teacher. You have wanted for some time to go to school and obtain a degree in teaching. Because of your circumstances, you've kept this desire a secret because it does not seem possible.

Wondering if it could ever happen keeps you from disclosing your desire to anyone for fear of ridicule. When you heard God's message assuring you that He intends to do it, you decided to believe that He would make it happen. That is your faith causing you to believe what God says—even when, on the surface, it seems highly improbable.

Now you have to apply your faith and expect it to bring the results of what you believe God to do. You can believe all day long, but without works you are not going to have what you desire. Faith without works is dead. It doesn't produce anything. Go ahead and make plans for when your blessing becomes a reality. Begin by doing some research to find the right school for you to attend.

Keep in mind that your faith is the substance of what you want. It is what you hold on to while you are waiting on God to open up a door for you. But you have to give God something to bless. It is putting your faith into action, showing Him that you believe it is going to happen. But until you can hold the object of your faith in your hand—see it, feel it, touch that degree—it is all a hope.

You know the hope will come true because you are resting in what He has already promised. Your faith represents the down payment of what you are hoping to receive. Hoping in God is a necessary component of trusting in Him.

Faith, hope, and trust in God together are the evidence that what you expect to happen will materialize. Remember that the process begins with our faith. It contains the action that connects us to God. Scripture reminds us of the vital importance of faith, *"Without faith it is impossible to please Him"* (Hebrews 11:6). Why is this so? Our first job is to please God in whatever we do. It translates into obeying God because that is how we please Him.

Therefore, God requires His children to be obedient. Parents should particularly understand this principle because we require our children to obey us. For example, let's say that when my children were young, I told my daughter to pick up a toy and she didn't do it. I could assume one of two things: either she didn't hear me or that she just didn't want to do it, so she simply ignored me. "Pick up the toy, and I mean it," I repeat. Again, she ignored me. This time, I know she heard me. How do you think that I felt? She was being disrespectful, wasn't she? Let's also say that I told her brother who was playing with her to pick up the toy, and he obeyed me.

With which one should I have been more pleased? Do I love my son any more than my disobedient daughter? No. But I would reward my son for his obedience and discipline my daughter. That discipline might simply be giving something to my son that I didn't give to her. The reward is based in the fact that I am pleased with the one who heard me, believed me, and obeyed what I said.

God is the same way. When He says something, He wants you to hear it, believe it, and act on it. Otherwise you have disrespected Him. Some people believe everything that God says and seek to please Him through their actions. God rewards them accordingly. Others believe a little of what God said and subsequently get fewer rewards. Still others don't believe at all and get nothing. Those who receive nothing don't need to be angry at those who have a lot. All we have to do is believe God and behave in accordance with His commands.

You may say, "I don't have much faith." That's fine. Act on the faith you do have. You can start with a little and still get results. Our Lord said that all we need is faith the size of a tiny seed (see Matthew 17:20). That means you don't need much faith; you only need enough to believe God. And God will honor it because He judges your heart. He knows you are struggling, and He also sees your faith—no matter how small you think that it is. He will come through for you. When you witness the answer to your prayer of faith it will encourage you to exercise your faith for bigger and bigger results.

The more you understand how faith in God operates the more you will be willing to put your faith in Him. It's a process in which you will be pleased to participate as you partner with God through your faith and obedience.

THE HABITS OF A GODLY WOMAN

Longsuffering

We are on a lifelong pursuit of pleasing God. No one promised that the journey through life would be an easy one. In fact, Jesus warned us that we would face trouble. Yet He knows that we can succeed because He personally gave us the tools that we need. One of the things we have at our disposal is called longsuffering; it is an attribute that reflects God's character in our lives.

Although it works to our advantage to be longsuffering, our culture doesn't value the trait, perhaps because it is inconvenient for people to become vulnerable by putting their emotions in compromising situations. Yet it is a characteristic of a godly woman.

God wants you to reap the benefit of His myriad blessing. We are blessed when we behave in ways that please Him. Therefore, His Word includes many prayers that are designed to encourage and strengthen your resolve to understand what He expects of us. As you read this prayer, ask the Holy Spirit to make it real to you so that it will manifest in your daily life: *"That ye might walk worthy of the Lord unto all pleasing, being fruitful in every good work, and increasing in the knowledge of God; strengthened with all might, according to his glorious power, unto all patience and longsuffering with joyfulness"* (Colossians 1:10–12 KJV).

The word *longsuffering* means patiently enduring a lasting offense or hardship. To achieve this quality, we need to get to know God in a very special way. You cannot follow someone's example, no matter how excellent it may be, unless you observe that person's actions. This is yet another reason to have an intimate relationship with our Lord. He will show us how to cope with the various conditions of life—even adversity. We get so many benefits from handling difficult situations with longsuffering, such as the power to achieve good works, the ability to demonstrate tolerance of others, and the overall satisfaction of knowing that God is pleased with us.

It is good to suffer long when there is a godly purpose for the suffering. So many biblical characters demonstrated the trait. For example, Hannah, a devoted woman of faith, spent years of longsuffering as she waited on God to bless her with a child. Throughout her days of barrenness, she was exposed to the ridicule of her husband's other wife. Although jealous of Hannah, the favored wife, Peninnah bore several offspring with the husband whom they shared. Because she seemingly had the upper hand, she loved to flaunt the fact that she had been blessed with children.

Scripture says that she made light of Hannah, reporting, *"Her rival, however, would provoke her bitterly to irritate her, because the Lord had closed her womb"* (1 Samuel 1:6). Apparently, Hannah silently suffered the taunting; the Bible does not record any retaliation on her part. Instead, she took her petition to God. After some time, He answered her prayer, and Hannah did receive a child from the Lord.

There are many others. But the greatest model of longsuffering is our Savior, Jesus. Teaching fickle crowds, enduring faithless disciples, and putting up with deserting followers, He suffered unto death.

How do you suffer for a long time without being destroyed in the process? Keep your relationship with God fine-tuned. Talk to Him about situations that trouble you and listen to what He has to say in return. Trust His guidance and know that He has your back. He will keep you from making rash decisions. He will also help determine when your suffering is not His will.

Take comfort in knowing that the Holy Spirit sets boundaries to protect us. Ask God, "How do You want me to handle this?" Study everything the Word says about the subject of godly suffering. Make sure you don't pick and choose Scriptures, or you can be misled to a faulty conclusion.

For example, Linda was an abused wife. Her husband attended church regularly. She did not attend church very often and thought most Christians were hypocrites. One Sunday, she decided to go. The sermon was based on the Scripture *"Wives, submit yourselves unto your own husbands, as unto the Lord"* (Ephesians 5:22 KJV). After the service, her husband said, "See, if you would submit to me and do what I tell you I wouldn't have to treat you the way I do."

It didn't make sense to Linda why her husband was so abusive. She knew that she followed his orders, but she could never do enough to please him. Linda had tried talking to God about it, but nothing had changed. She felt as if God was against her too. Unfortunately, her misunderstanding kept her estranged from Him.

Linda's husband was wrong. He misapplied the Scripture, bending it to suit his own selfish purposes. If you are being abused, God is not pleased. You can find comfort in His Word, which will tell you how precious and loved you are. Your husband or boyfriend may use the Bible to tell you how awful you are and that you will never amount to anything. He might tell you how Satan uses you or is in control of you. He might even try to convince you how righteous he is in comparison to you.

Recognize that as spiritual abuse. But don't be discouraged and give up on God. Your first line of defense is to pray and ask God to open your eyes and your heart to Him. He will always be there for you and will show you what to do. Then, if you have questions about His Word and need help in understanding it, consult a local minister that you believe you can trust. Most of all, know that God loves you for you.

As a final caution: beware of pride. Pride prevents longsuffering. Pride will tell you that you don't have to suffer at all. This is unbiblical and ungodly.

Temperance

Temperance is another word for self-control. The root word is temper. You can tell how temperate you are by how quickly you get an attitude. Some people get an attitude and think it is all right. They tend to blow up at the slightest provocation. Then they dismiss their behavior by saying, "I have an attitude today," and everybody seems to accept it. It is not okay. Sometimes I want to say, "Who gave you the right to make everybody miserable?"

I live in Dallas, and in the summer the temperature reaches over 100 degrees. Some people get an attitude and their tempers flare up because they are too hot! Conversely, I have to watch myself when I get cold. I hate being cold. So I tell myself, "Karia, don't get an attitude. You are just cold. You'll be all right." Then I operate on what I tell myself, not how I feel.

The apostle Paul put it this way, *"Not that I speak from want, for I have learned to be content in whatever circumstances I am"* (Philippians 4:11). Contentment is a learned behavior. By the grace of God, you practice it and perfect it. When you are fine with being hot or cold, whether things are going your way or not, whether you have what you think you need or don't, it will increase your self-control.

So be content with who you are. That is what God expects of you because being like God is our ultimate objective. Paul even taught that contentment goes hand in hand with godliness as he explained, *"Godliness actually is a means of great gain when accompanied by contentment. For we have brought nothing into the world, so we cannot take anything out of it either"* (1 Timothy 6:6–7). At the end of the day, it is what we do for God that will last.

Gentleness

If you've ever combed a little girl's hair and heard her say, "Ouch . . . that hurts!" you might have responded, "You are tender-headed." What you are telling her is that she is easily hurt when her head is treated with normal roughness. Many people are tender-*life*-d. Life has knocked them around, pulled on them, and hurt them. Maybe they feel as though they've reached their limit and need to see the gentleness of God's Spirit in you.

This is a good reminder to handle people with care. When people are faced with various adversities, you may never know what they are trying to cope with. They may need a kind word just at the moment you are crossing their path. So listen to the sound advice from God's Word, *"Let your gentle spirit be known to all men. The Lord is near"* (Philippians 4:5). When you are gentle, your care for people is reflected in how you behave toward them. God sees gentleness as the physical way that you show your goodness to others.

Goodness

Goodness is part of the new nature we are given as a result of receiving Christ as our Savior. It is an expression of the heart that is manifested through honest and just actions. Many Scriptures describe our Lord as good and upright. Therefore, your goodness is reflected in these honorable traits that are a product of the Holy Spirit. This is the only way that we can be genuinely good.

Therefore, goodness is not something a person can merely *try* to do. It is something the Holy Spirit grows inside of an individual who has been translated out of darkness by the Word of God. If God's Spirit is not influencing their deeds, people can do good things and not be good in the biblical sense of the word. Certainly there are acts of goodness that can and should be done. You can prepare a meal for someone in need, care for someone's children while they run errands, or teach someone to cook or sew.

Maybe you can offer a kind word to a discouraged soul or bring donuts to a social or business gathering. But these things within themselves are not goodness. Just remember that, without the Lord in your life it is not the Spirit of God who is directing you to do good works. Who you are as a result of integrating Christ into your life is what makes you good.

Meekness

My pastor, Dr. Tony Evans, describes meekness as strength under control.[5] I like that because it means that meekness is not wimpiness. Meekness is demonstrated when you accept the authority God gives so that He gets the results He wants. Being fully God, Jesus demonstrated meekness when He placed His strength under the control of the Father. He also pronounced a blessing over those who are meek, saying that they will inherit the earth (Matthew 5:5). You and I show meekness when, although strong, we submit our strength to a legitimate authority.

There are several forms of authority to which we are to submit. For example, if you are married, your husband is your legitimate authority. We must also obey the governmental laws in this nation, and children must submit to the authority of school officials. Then again there are certain forms of authority that we can choose to submit to.

I recently started a workout program. When I joined a new gym, I got a personal trainer. He tells me what to do. As I follow his instructions, I become stronger. In this case, I am accepting an authority that I chose in order to receive the results I want. While we are under various forms of authority we are to act in meekness. It is all a part of our divine design to follow Jesus' example of meekness.

On the other hand, meekness does not mean that you are a doormat. Sometimes people mistake a meek person for a weak person. Some will even try to intimidate you and make you feel inferior. It is all right to have a humble spirit; God is pleased when we show humility. But at the same time, you should recognize when you have a contribution to make.

God has gifted you and it is through Him that you are able to share your gifting with others. You cannot allow another person to suppress your gift by using intimidation. It is easy to think, *I'm not going to say anything. I'm not important anyway. What difference does it make what I think?* That is not meekness. Don't be afraid to offer input that may contribute to the successful outcome of a situation. Know that what you have to say is important.

THE COMMUNICATION OF A GODLY WOMAN

As godly women, we must be very mindful about how we communicate. So with the help of the Holy Spirit, we must take command of that tiny member of our bodies that can cause great trouble—the tongue. Scripture gives us the solution: seek wisdom from God. Only He can give us the ability to keep ourselves from saying something that may be damaging to others.

There are people who curse and say, "I'm trying to stop cursing." If they really wanted to stop cursing, they would. The Word of God admonishes us to *"let no corrupt communication proceed out of your mouth, but that which is good to the use of edifying, that it may minister grace unto the hearers"* (Ephesians 4:29 KJV). *Corrupt* means rotten, or putrefied. Something that is corrupt is worthless, of poor quality, bad, and not fit for use. Have you ever smelled rotten fish or rotten eggs? Nauseating, right?

When you open your mouth, God is not pleased if the words that come forth tear people down instead of building them up. That is nauseating as well. The Bible also tells us to be quick to hear, but slow to speak (see James 1:19). It also warns us to keep our tongues from evil (see Psalm 34:13). So before you speak, check to see if what you are going to say is wholesome and useful. If it is not, close your mouth and clean up your heart.

How do you make your words useful? Proverbs 16:24 can help: *"Pleasant words are a honeycomb, sweet to the soul and healing to the bones."* My mother used to say, "You can say anything you want, as long as you say it sweetly." That meant even when I had something negative to communicate, it would be better accepted if my words were kind. But also take into consideration Proverbs 25:11, that offers a lovely morsel of truth, *"Like apples of gold in settings of silver is a word spoken in right circumstances."*

Just because you think it, doesn't mean you have to say it. There is a lot of wisdom in knowing when to talk and when to be quiet. Speak only when your words help the person to whom you are talking, both in what you say and how you say them.

REJOICING IN YOUR DIVINE DESIGN

There is absolutely nothing wrong with a woman who is confident in herself when that self-confidence shows in her approach to life. For women, that means there are all sorts of fun things to do. And God applauds! Take shopping, for instance. Many women enjoy shopping and take pride in how good they are at shopping for bargains.

But please note: If you consistently pay too much for what you buy—including the credit card interest you pay, it would be a good idea to stop and take inventory of your shopping habits. Perhaps you could benefit from some counseling on consumer spending.

There was a woman in the Bible who was the mother of a king. King Lemuel's mom told her son in Proverbs 31 what kind of wife he should be looking for. At the beginning of the passage she tells him how valuable he is to her. Then she warns him against wasting his time chasing women. Many kings had wasted away their kingdoms by behaving unwisely. Instead, she wanted him to be good and generous and stand up for what is right. She also wanted very much for him to marry a woman with many virtues.

Things haven't changed that much today either. Similar to the way that you and I would advise our sons on what kind of woman to look for, this wise mother taught her son. She also had some criteria that she wanted his wife to meet. Her daughter-in-law should be kind, generous, hardworking, and trustworthy. She wanted her son's wife to be sensible and frugal, but also to know how to dress her children well and make them presentable. In other words, she didn't want her grandchildren to look raggedy! For that matter, she didn't want him to have a raggedy-looking wife either!

God gives us wisdom and creativity. That means we don't have to be wealthy to look our best. I remember when we were flat broke. Someone gave me a sewing machine. Making my own clothes was a good thing because it doesn't take much material to make a skirt. I realize this may not be the answer for everyone.

But as a suggestion, if you are experiencing difficult times in today's economy, you might think about trying your skills at sewing. It could work for you as a less expensive alternative to the high cost of buying nice clothing. There is nothing wrong with keeping up the appearances of you and your children. And a little of the good judgment God gives us can go a long way.

Written in the book of wisdom, Lemuel's mom provided some insightful words about how a wise woman functions in her family. According to the king's mother, a wife should be productive, perhaps participating in real estate investment or designing and marketing a clothing line. The prospective wife she envisioned would travel to a market some distance away to secure the best deals. Her daughter-in-law should be the kind who would say positive things about her husband. He shouldn't marry someone who would complain and tell everybody what a horrible husband he was.

Embedded in these verses are some legitimate activities that we can enjoy—guiltlessly. We can go shopping and stay as long as it takes to find the best bargains. We can engage in commercial enterprise and not be considered unbiblical. We can use our intellect to successfully run our own business. We can be charity leaders in our community.

Moreover, we don't have to worry about being criticized for spending too much money on our apparel, because we know how to make wise choices. From morning until night, we can find pleasure as we watch out for our family's best interest and encourage our husbands to be all they can be.

God has given His daughters a multitude of gifts and talents and

He wants us to use them. According to His divine design, He says, "Go for it!"

Beauty and the Beast:
Beating Satan at His Game

*K*aren was lonely. She and her husband had been fighting for several years. He was caustic and looked at her with disdain. She couldn't do anything right in his eyes. She had long since believed the rumors that there was another woman. Maybe that's why he treated her so badly. Karen didn't know what had gone wrong in their relationship, but she knew that she would have to survive this. She closed her eyes to pray.

Sitting at her desk, she leaned forward with her face cupped into her hands. Suddenly, she felt a gentle touch on her shoulder. "Are you all right?" Karen looked up to see her coworker standing over her. It didn't matter that he wasn't as attractive as her husband. All she knew was that his hand felt good on her shoulder. It meant that somebody cared. She prayed silently, *Lord, get this man away from me. This is not the time.* She smiled and said distantly, "Yes. Thanks for asking."

THE TEMPTATION TO TEMPT

As he walked away, Karen tried to turn her attention back to her work. But she couldn't stop thinking about him; she knew that if she asked him to lunch he would go. He was single and doing well. He had a nice swagger, and he seemed kind. She really wanted to talk. No, she really wanted to be held. His voice floated warmly through the air. He was on the phone only a few cubicles away. *Having lunch with him wouldn't be so bad*, she thought, as she looked in the mirror. She straightened her hair and reapplied her lipstick.

The computer screen reflected the time: 12:00 p.m. *Just go . . . Just go*, she told herself. But she didn't move. She glanced at the picture of her two children sitting on her desk. Closing her eyes, she arose from her seat and willed herself forward. Just then she heard him say, "Good-bye." He had just ended his call. Karen paused. She was tempted to tempt.

IF IT FEELS GOOD . . .

Satan is waiting for an opportunity to destroy your life. The problem is that because he is so good at being deceptive, he is hard to recognize. He approaches you at your most vulnerable time, drawing out your weaknesses. Playing skillfully, he lures you through your desires . . . your unmet needs . . . into his wicked pleasures. Momentarily, once you give in, you enjoy them. The taste seems incomparable. Then after you've eaten from his hand, your eyes open to the damage you have done. Caught in his web, with each twist to break away, your heart tears a little more. His laughter rings out as you writhe in pain, cloaked in embarrassment and shame.

Satan has a game plan. The Bible reveals it so you can protect yourself from him. Listen to a description of that plan as it could have taken place in Genesis, chapter 3. Adam and Eve lived in the Garden of Eden. Adam loved his wife passionately, and she loved him. He enjoyed spending time with her. She was so mesmerizingly beautiful.

One day they were wandering through the Garden, gathering fruit for their evening meal.

When Eve moved a distance away from her husband, a snake approached her. This was not uncommon; there were snakes throughout the Garden. It didn't even bother Eve when the snake started talking. Who knew what they would encounter in the Garden! Every day was an adventure. Beyond a doubt, they were striking creatures, but the difference between this snake and any other was ever so slight. Yet it was obvious that this one was smarter, more cunning, beautiful, and strangely unusual.

Notice that the first thing Satan did was strike up a conversation with Eve. He spoke in a language she understood. He was as smooth as an angel, clearly intelligent and intriguing. Having found a being with characteristics consistent with his own, Satan easily camouflaged himself. Scripture records his sweet words, *"Indeed, has God said, 'You shall not eat from any tree of the garden'?"* (Genesis 3:1).

When engaging in successful dialogue with Christians, many philosophers have since employed Satan's method: Step #1: Start by questioning the listener's understanding of God and His Word. Step #2: Say that God doesn't mean something that His Word actually does say. Step #3: Say that God means something His Word doesn't say. #4: Transfer the listener's allegiance to you.

How would the snake know what God had said? God had spoken directly to His highest form of earthly creation. Yet Eve did not pick up on the fact that it was unusual for the snake to question God. She did not stop and ask herself what was it about this animal? As far as she knew, neither she nor Adam had seen him before.

WHAT'S IMPORTANT?

The first thing Satan did was use persuasive talk. That is the same tactic he will use with you. He will often approach you by planting a thought in your mind. He might ask such questions as: "Will it really hurt if . . . ?" "Does God really want you to . . . ?" or, "Does the Bible really say . . . ?" He will take the Word of God and twist it to accomplish his objective; that is, to confuse you.

If you allow him to, he will cause you to question your biblical beliefs. Moreover, his appeal will be based on your desires. What is your weakness? What do you want? What do you think that you need? What is your current goal? In that area, Satan will use your desires against you and tempt you to disobey God's Word.

Satan wants you to disobey God by making you think that you are right. He entices you to decide that God's Word doesn't make sense in your situation. He wants you to think that Scripture allows room for interpretation beyond its true meaning. In doing this, he perverts your thinking so that you reason with yourself, "Surely, God wouldn't mind me getting a divorce under these circumstances." Even though you are aware of the biblical reason why God allows divorce, you still entertain the idea.

Jesus was very clear when He stated, *"And I say to you, whoever divorces his wife, except for immorality, and marries another woman commits adultery"* (Matthew 19:9). But you continue to justify your decision, "God wants me to be happy, right?" Wrong. Jesus also said, *"What therefore God has joined together, let no man separate"* (Matthew 19:6). In spite of your temptation to do otherwise, our Lord gave the acceptable reason for divorce—and your happiness is secondary to His Word.

Because of the danger that temptation presents, you must give serious consideration to God's Word before you decide to act. Let's say, for example, that someone you know is planning a party and all your girlfriends are going to be there. It happens to be your good friend's birthday, and it would be rude of you not to go. By the way, there will be a male stripper. But the other girls are Christians too, so it must be all right . . . this time. *It is all in good fun*, you tell yourself. You could even go into another room when the stripper is there. Yet, the Word says *"Abstain from every form of evil"* (1 Thessalonians 5:22). What do you decide to do? How do you reconcile what the Word tells you with the dilemma facing you?

In another example, you don't want to be intimate with your husband. The two of you have been arguing about bills for the better part of the day. Surely, God must understand that. Well, this is what the Word of God says about the situation: *"Be angry, and yet do not sin; do not let the sun go down on your anger"* (Ephesians 4:26). And 1 Corinthians 7:5 further advises, *"Stop depriving one another, except by agreement for a time, so that you may devote yourselves to prayer, and come together again so that Satan will not tempt you because of your lack of self-control."*

Now, if physical abuse is involved, that is an entirely different situation, which calls for a completely different approach. Other than that, it is better to obey the Word than to be OK with your excuses.

You would never overtly disobey God; your situation just happens to be an exception to the rule. If that is what you are thinking, know that Satan is talking. He will tell you what you want to hear. There is no compromise if what you are considering is in opposition to the Word of God. You are wrong, and God does not approve.

Although Satan's job is to draw out of you that which will tempt you, he has no original material. He has to use your own devices to defeat you. Scripture teaches, *"Let no one say when he is tempted, 'I am being tempted by God"; for God cannot be tempted by evil, and He Himself does not tempt anyone. But each one is tempted when he is carried away and enticed by his own lust"* (James 1:13–14). Satan's art is in holding up your desires to you and convincing you to act on them independently of God. When you do that, you invite destruction into your life that seldom stops with you.

Your actions would most likely cause a domino effect. Once you have fallen, others are affected when the pain you cause touches those who are closest to you. Sometimes your actions tempt others to follow in your path to destruction.

In the course of their conversation, Satan challenged Eve's belief in God. She eventually paid a high price for disobeying Him. Just because someone talks to you about God does not mean they are committed to His Word. They could be representing Satan in disguise. That is why it is so important to know the Word of God for yourself. Listen carefully. Note whether what you are hearing violates or questions the Word. When it does, Satan is talking.

EQUAL OR NOT?

Don't repeat the error of Eve's ways. She responded to Satan's verbal hook. Making a critical mistake, she decided to act independently of Adam and God. When she did, she made herself vulnerable. She was not designed to dominate her husband or to disobey her God. Yet that was the result of her actions.

At the same time, God did not create an inferior creature when He created Eve. She was created equal to Adam. She was made in God's image just as Adam was. The only difference was that Eve represented the divine design that God devised for her gender. She too had a mind, soul, and body. She was given gifts, skills, and abilities. But Eve was created *for* Adam.

When God gave Eve to him, Adam named her and took responsibility for her. She would be his friend and his companion, completing him in every way. Her strength would become his resource. His strength would become her protection. Together, as each maximized their abilities, they would work under Adam's loving administration to dominate their world. When Satan broke the partnership and violated the relationship, Adam wimped out—and Eve took charge.

I wonder what kind of pain God experienced as He watched the snake violate His creation. He must have wanted so badly for man to make the right choice and refuse Satan's bait. Yet, instead of taking charge and defending his woman from the attack, Adam went along with it. God waited to hear her cry for help, but she acted independently of Him.

The gut-wrenching moment rapidly approached, and God allowed them to make their choice. "Adam . . . say something, Adam. Eve . . . Don't fall for it, Eve. I love you." Heaven trembled. Eternity watched as the act of disobedience marred God's perfection. Did God glance at His Son? The spirit that would invade Judas flirted with the woman

He had created, and there was no defense for her. She would choose her enemy over her Creator. The first couple had succeeded in breaking their covenant with God.

The lesson to learn is that you must have sound knowledge of the Word of God. That was Eve's downfall when she attempted to repeat what God had told them. She said to Satan *"From the fruit of the trees of the garden we may eat; but from the fruit of the tree which is in the middle of the garden, God has said, "You shall not eat from it or touch it, or you will die"* (Genesis 3:2–3). Having a working knowledge of the Word of God is critical to obeying it. Eve misstated God's command, and Satan used it against her. Be very careful; he will do the same to you. Take responsibility for your knowledge of the Word and your obedience to it. Test yourself! Which of the following statements are not in the Bible?

If you take one step, God will take two
Cleanliness is next to godliness
To thine own self be true
God helps those who help themselves
The eye is the window to the soul
Better to cast your seed . . .
Pride comes before the fall
Money is the root of all evil

The answer is: none of them! Before we condemn Eve for not knowing the Word of God we need to look at ourselves. Eve didn't actually know what she thought she knew. Satan confused her mind, heart, and will because she did not know the Word.

Are you dealing with an issue in your life? Make sure you know what the Bible says about it. When you study His Word first, and talk later, you will be prepared to stand against the enemy. Remember what the Bible says, *"Be diligent to present yourself approved to God as a workman who does not need to be ashamed, accurately handling the word of truth"* (2 Timothy 2:15).

WHO'S IN CONTROL?

Satan's game plan is progressive, and he doesn't give up easily. The serpent directly contradicted God's Word when he told Eve, *"You surely will not die! For God knows that in the day you eat from it your eyes will be opened, and you will be like God, knowing good and evil"* (Genesis 3:4–5). First, Satan makes a logical proposal that entices you to question your understanding of the Word of God. Second, he argues his point, causing you to question your own judgment. Finally, he opposes God outright. This is the art of seduction at work. His objective is to become your god. When you are in cooperation with the devil, you abandon God's Word and follow the enemy's instructions.

One also sees this progression when a man seduces a woman. He begins by making her question her sound judgment. He stays over later than he should. He suggests, "Why shouldn't I?" They aren't doing anything wrong. The slippery slide toward seduction has already begun when she violates her own conscience and allows him influence over her decisions.

Finally, he tells her that he loves her and that they shouldn't wait. They've gone too far now, how could she tell him to turn back? He successfully begs himself into her bed. It starts with persuasive talking. It ends with his encouraging her to directly contradict God's command. Satan has spoken.

SATAN IS . . .

Know the enemy's tactics so that you can avoid his trap. Satan is the power behind anyone who comes to you presenting one agenda but really has a hidden, ungodly agenda. If you know the Word and you have an intimate relationship with God, as the conversation progresses, you can discern that the perpetrator's pleasant tone is a cover for an evil intent.

- Satan is the power behind anyone who makes you question your own ability to understand the Word of God and make moral decisions accordingly. When given the opportunity, he will make you doubt yourself and the honorable standards you have set for yourself.

- Satan is the power behind someone who presents himself as having direct knowledge from God that contradicts true knowledge gained from Scripture. Beware of people who will tell you, "The Lord told me to say this to you . . ." To expose the enemy's position, the Word of God instructs us in this manner, *"Beloved, do not believe every spirit, but test the spirits to see whether they are from God, because many false prophets have gone out into the world"* (1 John 4:1).

- Satan will ask questions that make you second-guess yourself. He may not directly tell you what to think. Instead, he influences your thoughts. As the conversation proceeds, he introduces an unbiblical perspective.

- Satan is the power behind anyone who presents you with a faulty interpretation of Scripture that you find appealing because it gives you permission to do what you know is wrong. The truth always has two sides: grace and judgment. A lie will deny one or the other. It will make you feel condemned when you have been forgiven, or provide a false sense of confidence to encourage you to do what you know you shouldn't. When you've made up your mind to choose sin, Satan will be present when you say to yourself, *God will have to forgive me for this . . . or God understands . . .*

- Beware of Satan's schemes when you hear someone say, "God wouldn't *really* want you to . . ." He is the power behind anyone who places himself in the position of authority over you when that right legitimately belongs to your husband or to the Lord. This is the girlfriend who says, "It's not your husband's place to . . ." or, "Your husband shouldn't . . ."

- Satan is the power behind anyone who head-on negates what God has said. This is the time to remember that the Word says, *"There is no wisdom and no understanding and no counsel against the Lord"* (Proverbs 21:30). Satan will use others to misrepresent the Word of God and convince you to sin, particularly when they know that you are unclear about what God has said.

Satan will attack the validity of God's Word and try to convince you that it doesn't apply to all situations. When you carefully consider all of these assertions, what is the area in your life where Satan is speaking?

BACK TO EDEN

As Scripture recorded the deadly deed: *"When the woman saw that the tree was good for food, and that it was a delight to the eyes, and that the tree was desirable to make one wise, she took from its fruit and ate; and she gave also to her husband with her, and he ate. Then the eyes of both of them were opened, and they knew that they were naked; and they sewed fig leaves together and made themselves loin coverings"* (Genesis 3:6–7).

Satan had successfully stirred within Eve the three areas of temptation that he uses: the lust of the flesh, the lust of the eyes, and the pride of life (see 1 John 2:16).

The Lust of the Flesh

Eve *"saw that the tree was good for food"* (Genesis 3:6). In other words, the fruit looked appealing. You experience the lust of the flesh when your body wants something that God has not authorized.

The lust of the flesh allows illegitimate approval to do something that makes you feel good. Satan even tempted Jesus with the lust of the flesh in Matthew 4:3. After Jesus had fasted forty days and forty nights, the tempter said to Him, *"If You are the Son of God, command that these stones become bread."* Jesus could have chosen to do it, His body may have wanted it, but God had not authorized it.

Since Jesus made all of His decisions according to the Word of God, He responded, *"It is written, Man shall not live on bread alone, but on every word that proceeds out of the mouth of God"* (Matthew 4:4). In other words He was saying, "I will eat when my Father God says I can eat." As followers of Jesus, we all need to eat when God says we can eat.

The Lust of the Eyes

"It was a delight to the eyes" (Genesis 3:6). The lust of the eyes is involved when we see something we want and we are tempted to access it illegitimately. Satan tempted Jesus with the lust of the eyes in Matthew 4:8. The passage reads, *"Again, the devil took Him to a very high mountain and showed Him all the kingdoms of the world and their glory; and he said to Him, 'All these things I will give You, if You fall down and worship me.'"*

The crux of the temptation was to determine who Jesus would worship. The Bible clearly states that we are to be content with what we have (see Hebrews 13:5). When God is at the center of our lives it is not so easy to be swayed by what we see. Have you seen anything you want that tempts you to disobey God? Maybe you have been watching some of the many television programs that display the lavish lifestyles of celebrities and other wealthy people. If you happen to follow these shows they might give you ideas about wanting a better house than the one that you have.

Some people enjoy watching the expensive automobiles promoted on various television shows and commercials. If you drive an older model, you might just begin to think that you deserve something better. You saw that car you've been dreaming of at the dealership last week. Somehow you'll make the payments . . . you tell yourself. Still others are tempted by exotic vacation brochures or a pair of pricey shoes you spotted while window-shopping.

I have something in my home that probably also belongs in yours. It is a little note that is a constant reminder to me, "Girls just want to have funds!" Girlfriends, obey God and stand strong against temptation. He is always right. But know that He will not compete for your affection. You have a free will, and you must take authority over the enemy just as our Lord did. Jesus responded to His temptation with great force, *"Go, Satan! For it is written, 'You shall worship the Lord your God, and serve Him only'"* (Matthew 4:10).

The Pride of Life

"And that the tree was desirable to make one wise" (Genesis 3:6). The pride of life appeals to a human tendency to want to exalt ourselves. We want to be more than we actually are by appearing to be wiser, richer, and more beautiful. When we strive to be admired by other people, we substitute people's admiration for God's approval.

Satan tempted Jesus with the pride of life. He took Jesus into the holy city and set Him up on the pinnacle of the temple. He then said to Jesus, *"If You are the Son of God, throw Yourself down; for it is written, 'He will command His angels concerning You'; and 'on their hands they will bear you up, so that you will not strike your foot against a stone'"* (Matthew 4:6).

Let me break this down to our reality. In other words, Satan goes to church with some of us, and he tempts us to show off for all the church folk. He says, "Here's your audience. Prove to us who you are." The pride of life shifts the focus from God and turns it toward men. Ask yourself, who is the audience for your life—God or man? If you are honest with yourself, the answer to that question will tell you how susceptible you are to the pride of life.

Actually, it's quite easy to switch audiences. When your friends are your audience, you concern yourself with thinking, *What will my friends think of how I look? Do I fit in?* Then again, your husband can be your audience. Scripture teaches that you will want to please him (see 1 Corinthians 7:34) and that is understandable. Still, you cannot make him your God.

Instead of trying to please everyone else but God, the goal should be to imitate our Lord. Jesus answered Satan, *"It is written, you shall not put the Lord your God to the test"* (Matthew 4:7). The word "test" also means to tempt. It is the idea of testing in order to prove. In other words, don't ask God for something so that you can show off who you are. On a personal level, you may want a slimmer figure, a better wardrobe, or more prestigious friends so you can be admired by people who see you. You expect God to bless you so people can admire you. That is the pride of life, and it is a sin.

DANGER! DANGER!

Giving in to temptation is a most dangerous endeavor. If you know something is true because God said it, you must settle in your heart that you will do it. Otherwise, you are in a state of indecision, and that is the womb of sin. Entertaining an idea that could possibly make you look good to someone, you want to lie—and you know it is wrong. But you have not decided that you will not lie. Instead you are tempted to do so. The same principle applies to cheating, unbiblical relationships, and illegitimate sexual relationships. Avoid letting how you feel be the authority for your decisions. Allow God's Word to dictate your direction.

The passage in Matthew chapter 4 concludes with Jesus having victory over Satan. He never gave in to sin. He offered God a sinless sacrifice, and, as such, He is the only One who qualifies to be our Savior. For anyone who wants to be obedient to God, the Word of God provides the way, *"If you confess with your mouth Jesus as Lord, and believe in your heart that God raised Him from the dead, you will be saved; for with the heart a person believes, resulting in righteousness, and with the mouth he confesses, resulting in salvation"* (Romans 10:9–10).

If you would like to accept Jesus right now as your personal Savior, pray this prayer: *"Lord, you said in Romans chapter 10, verses 9 and 10 that if I confess with my mouth that you are Lord, and believe in my heart that God the Father raised You from the dead, that I will be saved. Lord, I am doing that right now. I confess with my mouth that You are Lord. I believe in my heart that You have risen from the dead. Therefore, I thank*

You for saving me and changing my life forever." If you prayed this prayer for the first time, congratulations! You are now God's child. Welcome to the family of God![6]

ACCESSING YOUR DIVINE DESIGN

Yes, it was through our gender that death entered the world. But so did life. A woman was used of God to bear His Son—my Savior and yours. If a finger is pointed at the woman for introducing sin, it must also point at her for birthing Jesus. God cleared our name and our reputation. His love has redeemed us. Jesus is our honor.

Now build a wall between you and temptation so that you will always bring honor to our Lord. Here are the bricks:

- Develop your prayer life. Communicate with God before the temptation, so you will recognize it when it comes.
- Watch for the approach of temptation. Don't position yourself to fall into sin.
- Don't talk to the devil. The longer you entertain thoughts by him, the more reasonable he begins to sound.
- Know God's Word. The Word of God is the sword of the Spirit. It will cut through the confusing options Satan presents you.
- Call for help when you are in over your head. If you are married, talk to your husband. He is to be the spiritual leader in the home. Develop accountability relationships with godly women who can help you straighten out your thinking. Don't try to fight temptation by yourself.
- Obey God's Word. See your success.

You are designed to defeat your enemy. Access your divine design to achieve victory over temptation—and enjoy being a woman!

Single and Significant

Sharon was formerly a pastor's wife. God has since redeemed her from the tragic circumstances that led to her divorce. One day she was visiting an old friend, and the two of them had a chance to catch up. They hadn't seen each other in over a year. Sharon told her friend about the amazing things that God is doing in her life. She is the women's minister at her new church and feels a strong calling to help hurting women. She said, "Maria, I've gone through it. But God is using every bit of what I experienced for His good."

As Maria continued to listen, Sharon shared so much. She heard the voice of a woman who looks in the mirror and says, "Sharon, you are an awesome mom. You go, girl!" As a single mother, she has learned to encourage herself. Maria heard the voice of a provider who has learned the secret of financial security. Sharon said, "I get so excited when there are no options, because I have learned that is when God comes out of nowhere and blows my mind!"

Maria also heard the voice of a prayer warrior whom God wakes up in the wee hours of the morning and reminds her to trust Him. "Don't worry, Sharon. Don't be surprised at what happens today. Remember, I'm in control and I have a plan." Most of all, Maria heard the voice of a woman who was no longer looking for her identity in a mate. Sharon continued, "Many women say, 'I'll be happy when I find a husband.' I say to them, 'No, you won't. If you're not happy by yourself, you won't be happy with somebody else. You have to first find your identity in Christ. Then whoever comes along can be an addition. If they are a subtraction, they've got to go because you don't need them in your life to validate you.'"

This was the voice of a woman who would love to have a mate but who has learned the secret of how to be single and significant.

A SINGLE SET OF INSTRUCTIONS

Sharon's words address a common problem. If your status is any of the following: never married, divorced, or widowed—it is possible to feel incomplete and unfulfilled without a mate. You might also be tempted to look for your identity and security in a relationship. Naturally, there are times when you might desire another human being in your life who recognizes your value, who will share life's experiences with you, or who will affirm you and make you feel complete.

For those who are unmarried, know that there is a single set of instructions for you that is found in 1 Corinthians, chapter 7. When you are feeling like you are deficient without a husband, the apostle Paul addressed the proper conduct for you.

> *"Yet I wish that all men were even as I myself am. However, each man has his own gift from God, one in this manner, and another in that. But I say to the unmarried and to widows that it is good for them if they remain even as I. But if they do not have self-control, let them marry; for it is better to marry than to burn with passion."* (1 Corinthians 7:7–9)

I Wish That All Men Were Like Me . . .

Scripture reveals what Paul's character was like. Clearly, from his own words we find that he was focused on his calling. In fact, Paul considered his unmarried status as a benefit for him, rather than a problem. There are some people today who are like Paul. For these people, being married would be a distraction. They are so committed to their calling that they focus on living a life that transcends the earthly issues of marriage and family. To some degree they might faintly desire a family, but their calling fulfills them.

The benefits of this kind of life are quite marvelous; they prompted Paul to wish that everyone had this gift. But everybody doesn't have the gift, and Paul recognized that fact. So the question for us is, if Paul was unmarried and satisfied, how did he get that way? Further, is it possible for people in today's world to be unmarried and satisfied? The fact is that, most of the time we struggle because we are definitely not satisfied.

Each Man Has His Own Gift from God . . .

If you say, "I understand all that. But I still want to be married. Am I unfocused or distracted? Am I not in love with Christ?" Paul responded to these questions when he said, *"Each man has his own gift from God"* (1 Corinthians 7:7). The phrase "his own" pertains to one's self. In other words, Paul is saying that you have a gift that belongs to you. God gave some people the gift to be unmarried. Other people have other gifts. If after prayer and fasting you believe in your spirit that God desires for you to have a mate, believe Him for one.

When you pray about a mate, ask God what He wants for you. Pray, "God, do You want me to have a mate?" You can always present your requests before Him, but it is good to know what He has planned for you. Think seriously about how having a mate would benefit God. Some people get a mate and stop going to church regularly, stop serving, and stop pursuing what God called them to do. I can't believe that God is pleased with that.

One in This Manner, and Another in That . . .

The gifts that God gives each of us vary according to every individual. God did not make cookie-cutter people, or design cookie-cutter plans for His children's lives. That is what Paul meant when he said, *"One in this manner, and another in that"* (1 Corinthians 7:7). Sometimes even Christians don't understand this principle. They will ask questions and make comments such as, "When are you going to get married?" or, "You'd better get married soon; your eggs are going to dry up." How hurtful!

However, Paul would say to them, *"Only, as the Lord has assigned to each one, as God has called each, in this manner let him walk and so I direct in all the churches"* (1 Corinthians 7:17). He is reemphasizing that everybody has her own gift. Some people have the gift to remain unmarried, and other people are called to be married. God decides who gets what gift. Moreover, He is the God of time; He is in control. When people say you should be married by now, it is not their place to determine your gift. They could be disagreeing with God. And who are they to do that?

Paul addressed this message to the entire church, indicating everyone's responsibility to maximize their own gifts. The focus of the church is not to find mates for unmarried believers. But some may say, "If I don't meet someone at church, where will I meet him?" It's great to meet someone at church. It is just not the church's goal or duty to help you meet somebody. In God's plan, marriage is not the objective; walking according to your calling is. Then, along the way to your destiny, if you are to have a destiny partner—you will have one.

If God has called you to be married, keep your eyes open for a mate. Follow God's Spirit, and He will lead you where you need to go. He will make sure you are introduced to someone that He wants you to meet. Use His eyes to evaluate potential marriage mates. Make decisions according to His direction. Purpose in your heart that it is all about Him. If you honor Him, you will get the benefits.

If you are praying for a mate, listen first. Because today, this day, God has something He wants you to do that has nothing to do with being married. Become engrossed in obedience and see how God works it out.

But If They Do Not Have Self-Control, Let Them Marry . . .

I was talking to a young woman recently who was describing her struggle with the young man she was dating. She said, "Karia, there are times when we were together or just talking on the phone when I burn with such passion that I would like to scream out, 'Somebody bring a fire truck and hose me down!'" Paul says that if you are on fire, get married. Why? Because it is better to marry than to burn.

The word "better" means more useful, serviceable, or more advantageous. The Greek word for "burn" is *pyroo*. Together, these words mean to burn with fire or to set on fire. It is the same root word from which we get the word *pyrotechnics*, or explosive firecrackers. When you are "burning" with passion, you are completely out of control, you are on fire, and your brain is shooting off ignited signals.

Paul explained that it is more useful for you to be married than to be a walking firebomb. If quenching the fire of flashing red lights and sirens would be a relief to you, you might need to put a ring on it. If you are on fire and it is not for Jesus, that's when you know you need to get married. Marriage is the only acceptable fire extinguisher. If you try to put it out with any other extinguisher, it only makes the consequences of your fire worse the next time around—and there will be a next time.

You ask, "What if the fire is just for one person?" What if you are not normally on fire; it's only a problem when you are around this particular person? First of all, you should be dating another Christian. If you are in a relationship with him, make sure you meet him in accountable environments. Decide not to be alone together. Spend time on the phone rather than with each other (and watch your language while you are on the phone). Communicate via text messages. When you do go out, double-date. Meet over at someone's home.

A good test of his commitment to you is whether he can tell himself no and watch out for your interest over his. That is true even when you are not properly watching out for your own interests. If your urges persist, though, start thinking about getting married. If this man is not an appropriate marriage partner, you need to get away from him. If he is not God's man for you, he can destroy your life because you are not living in obedience to God's will and direction.

Don't fool yourself into thinking he's going to change. He's probably not going to. He might appear to change to get what he wants, but it will not be a lasting change. If you are not conducting your relationship in obedience to God, your discernment is dull. How will you know if he is tricking you? Ask the Holy Spirit to give you the grace that you need to move out of your desires and into God's will for you. You will survive it.

Afterward (yes, maybe a long time later), you will be able to see why. This brings to mind the age-old gospel hymn "We'll Understand It Better By and By" by Charles Albert Tindley. An old mother at my church used to sing this heartfelt song, *By and by, when the morning comes, when the saints of God are gathered home, we'll tell the story how we've overcome, for we'll understand it better by and by.*[7] Be obedient to the Word of God and the Spirit of God. You'll understand it better by and by.

You say, "That's easier said than done." There are a lot of things that are easier said than done. Finishing high school is easier said than done. Getting a college degree is easier said than done. Getting a job is easier said than done. Starting a business is easier said than done. You do things because that is the best thing for you. Just because something is "easier said than done" doesn't mean you don't need to go ahead and do it. Doing it is a decision of the will. Make the decision.

If you are thirty years old or under, let me offer this "pyrotechnic" test for you. To avoid making trouble for yourself, you might want to get married:

- If you are in the grocery store and you notice an attractive man. The thought runs through your head *Mmm, he has a nice body.* You let your imagination run wild as it gets deeper than a mere glance. You wonder what it would be like to look into his eyes.

- If you pull into a drive-through restaurant parking lot and catch a glimpse of a man also parking. You circle the parking lot at least one more time so you can look again. You spend the next hour or so fantasizing about him.
- If you watch football just to see muscular men run around in tight uniforms, absorbing the physical impact of them hitting each other, enjoying the ripples of their body as they run like rockets.
- If you just left church service and are talking to a man in the foyer. You are thinking, *Gee, it would be nice to . . .* or, *I wonder what it would be like to . . .* You keep having to repent because it continues to happen.
- If, even when you are alone with a guy you don't like, you start to feel uncontrollable sexual desires. You begin to think, *What's wrong with me?* But you still feel them, at least until you are no longer alone with him.

All right, enough of that!

SINGLE AND SATISFIED

We often use the word "single" in reference to those who are not married. However, the word Paul used in 1 Corinthians 7:8 is "unmarried." The root word is *gamos*, which simply means a wedding or marriage festival, a wedding banquet, or a wedding feast. In other words, an unmarried person in God's sight is simply one who has not had a wedding festival. There is no hint of being "single" and "alone" in the biblical view of marriage. The unmarried woman is to live within the context of an intimate relationship, just like the married woman. The only difference is her partner in intimacy.

When a woman is married, her intimate partner is to be her husband. For the unmarried woman, she is to surround herself with an environment where everything is a constant reminder that God is with her. That includes relationships with her immediate family members, her church family, and godly friendships that support her.

Moreover, developing godly relationships take time. Take the time to foster relationships in which your brother's and/or sister's children are like your own children. The person who sits behind you in church is like a second mother to you. You may even find young people whom you can mentor. For example, all of my children are of the age where they could be seriously dating or married. Yet God has not given them a mate. Since I wanted a grandchild, I decided that I would "adopt" one.

There is a wonderful young lady whom I love, and she happened to be pregnant at the time. One day I walked up to her and said, "When you have your baby, it is going to be my grandchild until such time as the Lord gives me one." She smiled (I just love her smile) and agreed. So now I have a beautiful baby boy that I can spoil rotten. It's great! And I am satisfied.

God wants that for you. Married or not, we are to be in genuine relationships with other believers. If you do not have an immediate family, He wants you to decide to develop relationships where you can spend the night on Christmas Eve. If otherwise you'd be alone, God wants you to wake up Christmas morning among loving people sharing with one another.

Furthermore, God wants you to go home after work and get in the bed exhausted from sharing His love with others, not exhausted from emotional isolation. It is possible, and you can do it. God wants you to have a place where you belong. There is probably somebody whom you know that would be so glad if you would enter her life in a significant way. Maybe not everybody, but somebody.

Paul was unmarried, but he wasn't alone. He allowed people into his heart. At the end of the letter he wrote to the church at Rome, he greeted Priscilla and Aquila. They were so close that they risked their lives for him. He also greeted house churches (which were small and intimate), other close friends, people that helped him plant churches, friends converted before him, mother figures, and entire families. Before he ended his letter, Paul had greeted more than sixteen people by name.

The same pattern is repeated in other letters Paul wrote. He was an unmarried man who belonged to the body of Christ; and the body of Christ belonged to him. Paul found complete fulfillment in his calling. His daily activity of preaching and teaching wasn't a job for him, it was a life. He wrote of his passion, *"For to me, to live is Christ and to die is gain"* (Philippians 1:21). He was so committed to Christ and his calling that everything else paled in comparison.

YOUR BLINDING ENCOUNTER

Paul's perspective on life was changed through a blinding encounter with Jesus. He had been religious-minded to a fault. With fierce determination, Paul secured letters from the high priest that authorized him to execute house-to-house searches in pursuit of Christians. Upon their capture, he would bind and drag his chained and crying captives to Jerusalem to be persecuted and put to death. The dirt road between safety and senseless brutality was their middle passage.

This was Paul's way of honoring God. He firmly believed that he was carrying out the will of God. His harmful deeds speak to the fact that a people can be sincerely wrong in their actions all the while they believe they are justified. But the truth is, if God could use Paul, He can use you.

When Paul was on the road heading to Damascus, a blinding light suddenly appeared. Jesus spoke to him, calling Paul by his Hebrew name, *"Saul, Saul, why are you persecuting Me?"* (Acts 9:4). Paul was blinded by the light and responded in verse 5, *"Who are You, Lord?"* Then, Jesus identified Himself and instructed Paul on what he should do.

To change the way you think about being unmarried, you need a blinding encounter with God. Religion won't do. Going to church won't do. You need a life-changing encounter with Jesus so you can submit your desires to Him. When you trust Him, you can submit to Him. Many of us do not trust Him, we are not submitting, and life is beating us up. Give it up. When you trust Him, you will seek His face and ask the question, "Lord, what will You have me to do?"

When Paul arose, he was actually blind. The King James Version says, *"he saw no man"* (Acts 9:8). I wonder what he saw in his mind. I can't help but think that the event he had just experienced was replaying in his mind. He must have struggled to comprehend what had just happened. He probably reflected on his past in light of his new revelation about the God he served.

Paul was blind, but not distracted. The challenge we have is that, even when we experience God in a powerful way, we are not "blinded" by that experience. In some cases, too many of us "Christians" celebrate in church on Sunday and by Friday night we are already distracted and ready to go to the club. We watch people take holy wedding vows and later get drunk at the reception. Strangely, the church, unholy activities, and the flirting men that we encounter can peacefully and easily coexist in our lives.

Thank God, you are not that extreme. However, there are those who desperately want a mate. They leave the sanctuary saying, "Yes, God." But at the same time they can't help envying the couples gathered in the foyer, because they want to be like them. It can be so difficult to accept God's will and His timing, can't it?

If you have had a similar experience, you are not alone. Many people struggle with waiting on God. But, at this point in your life, it would help if you remember that God has given you all that you need in order to be what He has called you to be. Being dissatisfied with what He has already provided is nothing less than sin. I am not saying that to desire a mate is a bad thing. But at the same time, to be dissatisfied until you get one is the same as being ungrateful for what you do have.

Paul was miraculously delivered from his blindness when God spoke to His servant Ananias and told him to lay hands on Paul. Ananias was hesitant because he knew of Paul's vicious reputation. But God said to him, *"Go, for he is a chosen instrument of Mine, to bear My name before the Gentiles and kings and the sons of Israel; for I will show him how much he must suffer for My name's sake"* (Acts 9:15–16).

You see, God had chosen Paul for his destiny before he was even born. There was nothing Paul could do that was bad enough for God to give up on him. Like Paul, God has a plan for you. No matter what you have done that is displeasing in God's sight, your plan is still in place. Go ahead, experience your blinding encounter with Christ and see what awaits you.

Paul had been an evil and despicable man toward believers in Christ. But when he met Jesus, God turned all that around. Because of his former mean character, he was super-sensitive to all of God's people. Now that he had seen both sides, he could identify with the oppressors and wanted to turn them toward the truth. At the same time, he hurt for the oppressed because he knew they were innocent. For His glory, God used even Paul's time of persecuting His people; Paul was perfectly prepared for his destiny.

Whether you realize it or not, you are perfectly prepared for your destiny. To help you understand what God has done for you, take some time and reflect on your past. He will help you see the seeds of what He will do for you in the future. God will use everything you have been through for His glory and your benefit.

As I read the account of Paul's new life in Christ, I am astounded by how much he endured. His future was not to be a bed of roses. For the sake of Christ, he was beaten and flogged, betrayed and imprisoned. There constantly seemed to be another trial, another beating, another imprisonment, or another incident of suffering waiting for him. As he had once persecuted others, Paul would be persecuted. According to historical tradition, ultimately he was beheaded.

Sometimes in life, there seems to be one troubling incident after another. We wonder when we will finally "get there." But you need to understand that you *are* there. Through your tests and trials, God is making you who He needs you to be. Keep seeking Him diligently and you will find your way. God never intended the journey to your destiny to bypass tribulations. Just as a potter who molds a piece of clay into a vessel worthy of fulfilling a specific function, God places you and me on the Potter's wheel to help us conform to His purpose. It is a painful process, but He will see us through it.

We should all join in Paul's declaration. When he found his identity in God, he declared, *"For I am convinced that neither death, nor life, nor angels, nor principalities, nor things present, nor things to come, nor powers, nor height, nor depth, nor any other created thing, will be able to separate us from the love of God, which is in Christ Jesus our Lord"* (Romans 8:38–39).

If you are single right now and desire a mate, this is a time that God has preordained for you. The question is: what does He want you to do? I will tell you this, if you are suffering, it is a part of your journey that will draw you closer to God. Say yes to God and let Him guide you into your moment of destiny. Let Him fulfill the design that He has made for your life.

When Paul's eyes were opened, he made preparations to begin his journey. First, he ate. Then he spent a few days with the disciples. After that, he started preaching Christ in the synagogues (see Acts 9:18–20). Paul didn't waste any time talking about his experience. He didn't sit around and debate what he should do either. He immediately did what God told him to do. What have you been called to do? It is time for you to do it. Quit debating. Obey God.

I don't know what that first synagogue service was like after his conversion, but I'm certain that Paul was fired up when he got there. He knew that he had given up his former life when he walked into the place of worship, and he was ready. Maybe when you walked into church on the day you accepted Christ, you didn't know you were giving up life as you once knew it. Maybe even today, you are struggling with fully surrendering to our Lord.

Sisters, complete surrender is required for you to maximize your experience with God. You may be thinking that is what was required of Paul, but you don't see such a radical move as a requirement for yourself. To you, Paul would say, *"Therefore I urge you . . . by the mercies of God, to present your bodies a living and holy sacrifice, acceptable to God, which is your spiritual service of worship"* (Romans 12:1).

Here Paul is admitting that you can only give up your life by God's mercy. He has to give you the grace on the inside of you so that you can give up everything on the outside of you. When you ask Him, He will give you that grace. There is no shortcut in the Christian life. Relationships develop over time when it comes to building them with other people and with God. As you develop your intimacy with Him, you will fall so much in love with Him that you will be willing to give up anything for Him. Just like Paul, you will care more about His happiness than you do your own. That's when it becomes a joy to submit.

Have you ever played the game where you stand in front of someone, close your eyes, and fall backward? The person behind you is supposed to catch you. They call this a "team-building" exercise, and the purpose of it is to build trust between team members. God wants to do a team-building exercise with you. He wants you to close your eyes and learn to trust that He will catch you before you fall.

Many people are miserable because God is calling them, saying, "Let's be a team." But they are having trouble surrendering to Him. They're not so sure that they can trust God enough and let go of all the things in their lives that they depend on for support. Some people feel as though they can trust Him only to a degree. But when it's something they think they can handle on their own, the temptation to take matters into their own hands takes over. In essence they are saying to God, "It's okay. I can handle this. I don't need to fall back on You."

God sends word that it's all right to turn things over to Him, but you keep standing up on your own two feet. Let go, and let God take control. Fall back when He gives you direction, trusting Him to catch you. In your unmarried state, you can trust Him. In your finances, you can trust Him. In His plan for your life, you can trust Him. Fall back on His Word. Fall back on His promises. Fall back into the plan for your divine destiny. He's there. He won't let you hit the ground.

You may have a problem with trusting someone else; but you can trust God to catch you. He gives you a strong promise, and you can be sure that He is able to keep it, *"For He will give His angels charge concerning you, to guard you in all your ways. They will bear you up in their hands, that you do not strike your foot against a stone"* (Psalm 91:11–12).

FLIP THE SCRIPT

"The woman who is unmarried, and the virgin, is concerned about the things of the Lord, that she may be holy both in body and spirit; but one who is married is concerned about the things of the world, how she may please her husband." (1 Corinthians 7:34)

When Paul told the believers that it is better to be unmarried, he flipped the script on the world's view of sex and marriage. Why did Paul say this? He put God first—above all earthly concerns. He explained that there is a difference between a wife and a virgin. He said that the unmarried woman cares about the things of the Lord; she can be focused on how she can please the Lord through her holiness. However, because marriage is an earthly matter, a married woman must understandably care about the things of the world. She has to please her husband.

Paul's statement is based on his desire for all believers to maximize their devotion to God. His main goal is to teach the believers to live their lives according to the way that God has called them. When a woman is not married she has the freedom to go and come as she pleases. God has access to her time. When such a woman desires to please God, she can go to church anytime and serve as she is needed. She can go on mission trips and be active in ministries and para-church organizations. Her focus is completely on serving the Lord, and her heart is undivided.

So then, what does this mean to you? Paul is presenting a principle that says if you are called to be an unmarried woman, your time belongs to God. As you engross yourself in your calling, you find sufficiency in Him. You are free to be steadfast in accomplishing what God desires of you. You can work all night and all day if it pleases the Lord. If you choose not to, you don't have to cook dinner, be a companion to a mate, or alter your schedule to accommodate your spouse. Paul says that this freedom is beneficial to the kingdom of God—and it is a freedom you give up if you are married.

RELATIONSHIPS: ALONE, BUT NOT LONELY

What about the problem of feeling incomplete? Many women do feel this way. Adrienne Pluss, a talented young spoken word artist at my church, wrote a heartfelt poem entitled, "From the Heart of a Woman." She describes the thought process that women go through to discover that even in our loneliness we are not alone—God is with us all of the time. An excerpt of her poem reads:

LATELY, I'VE BEEN READING THROUGH MY JOURNALS
. . . my journeys . . . my prayers.
Reading through the years, I've become very aware,
That having a husband has been one of my number one cares.
There seems to always have been someone who caught my stares.
My attention has frequently diverted to a man who
seemed to be interested,
Even when I tried to fight against getting myself
. . . my heart . . . too invested.

THIS IS THE AREA I AM CONSTANTLY TESTED.
Molested . . . by thoughts of potentiality
Fantasy clouding my mentality.
Yes, I fantasize as though it could one day be actuality.
But it is just a way to escape the harsh reality
That I am alone . . . I feel alone.
Even though I've known
That God has proved
That He will not be moved
From His love for me
I still cling to wanting a man to release me.
A real life testament . . . that man will personify that God loves me.

BUT ALL I'VE EXPERIENCED ARE BEAUTIFUL PICTURES PAINTED IN LIES.
I blow up this bubble and refuse to see anything but blue skies.

Until I look in the mirror and draw myself nearer to see clearer,
That I am still one woman looking for something aesthetic
To keep me from examining the part of me that feels pathetic.
. . . not good enough for anyone to truly love.
At my core, there is a part of me that feels like I
will never be good enough.

*T*HIS IS A CONFINING LIE THAT I HAVE FOUND.
Now, instead of it holding me . . . the lie must be bound.
Because God has found a way to love me
It is in His nature to love me unconditionally.
And I beg for it in my deepest despondency . . .

*T*HIS IS WHAT I NEED. THIS IS THE PIECE THAT IS MISSING.
My worth is not wrapped up in hot and steamy kissing.
Bottom line, no matter how fine a man may be
Or how special and beautiful I feel when he looks at me
God is begging for me to see and experience the love He has for me.[8]

Adrienne is right. God is the answer to our insecurity, our need, our loneliness. If loneliness leads you into the arms of God, it is productive. But, at the same time, if you are not careful, loneliness can lead to idolatry. It can cause you to change your focus from God to a man. Then there is the possibility that you will try to manipulate God to get the object of your desire.

If that need for having a man in your life becomes an idol that you have elevated above God and He does not give you a man, you feel like He hasn't met your need. The real problem is not that you don't have a man. The problem is that you are misguided in your quest to fulfill your perceived need.

"Why do you say that?" you ask. God says that He will provide all your needs. But when you refuse to be satisfied without a man in your life, you are saying, "God, there is something I need that You have not provided. And I am not going to be happy until You do." In effect, you have shifted your focus from pleasing God to desiring a mate. And God wants to be the focal point in your life.

This is how it can work. When you idolize a vision of marriage, it has become the answer to your happiness. From that point Satan can keep you strung out for a long time. There are so many physical and spiritual factors he can manipulate. Most often to your detriment, he can bring "potential" people in and out of your life. Satan controls your feelings and undermines your trust in God. Your prayer changes from, "God, what do You want?" to, "God, will You give me what I want?"

You start to fantasize about the man you desire—he is your idol. When you believe that a man will heal your hurts, wipe away your tears, comfort you when you are sad, and rejoice when you are glad, that image of a man has taken the place of God in your life. For only God can truly satisfy all of your needs.

On the other hand, what if God finally gives you what you want? Will you wonder why you got tricked if the man you marry doesn't meet your needs? If you are disappointed, will you get mad at God and ask Him: "How could I have trusted You and waited this long, and You give me a man like this? He leaves his underwear on the floor, and he doesn't put the toilet seat down. He's late for dinner and doesn't call. He hasn't fixed the pipe under the sink for a year. He is insensitive, lazy, absent, broke, and mean." Well, he may have been your choice and not God's choice for you. Sometimes, as they say, you have to be careful what you ask for.

Ladies, if you aren't satisfied with Christ now, you won't be satisfied with a husband later. What is the solution? It is found in an old hymn. The words ring, "All to Thee, my blessed Savior, I surrender all. I surrender, I surrender all."[9] Let this be your daily prayer if you are to be unmarried and significant.

LET'S GET REAL

Being unmarried can be difficult, and our culture today doesn't help. Instead of promoting how unmarried people can enjoy and maximize their lives, the media focuses on the urgency of mating. It definitely doesn't encourage sacrificial love; instead, it's all about instant gratification. No real help is given on how to make a marriage work long term or how to give genuine unselfish affection—just mating.

Romance movies portray the female character living "happily ever after" with a rich and wonderful husband who loves her desperately. In the fast-action car movies, some gorgeous girl sits on the back of a Denzel look-alike's motorcycle and rides off into the sunset. "Single-oriented" television shows feature women who sleep with men to whom they are not married (and who are often someone else's husband). Such programs portray sassy women who fantasize about men, chase after them, or downgrade them. The featured scenes glorify sex, lies, and greed.

The message is—if you are funny, smart, or beautiful—you can get a hunk of a man. If you think you're none of those things, oh well, too bad for you. However, you can get someone, though, if you're willing to do all the "right things." Somebody made that stuff up and sold it to the television networks. Scandal sells. Now the studio is selling it to you. Don't buy it. God has your destiny in His hand. Follow Him, and He'll lead you to the place of your greatest fulfillment.

SURVIVING YOUR SURRENDER

Paul also talked about how to survive the experience of surrendering to Christ. He says, *"Brethren, each one is to remain with God in that condition in which he was called"* (1 Corinthians 7:24). The key is in the phrase *"with God."* God must become everything to you—your father, your friend, your comforter, your companion, and the object of your desire. You must be able to go on a date with Him and enjoy it. You must be able to eat dinner with Him and find Him a delightful companion. He must be the one you long to go home and be alone with.

These positive results only come by spending time with Him, learning what He is like, being able to sense when He is happy or upset, being able to laugh and smile together. You must be able to do this and mean it—not exercising your will in such a way to manipulate Him for an ulterior motive. Remember, God sees your heart.

It's important to note that marriage doesn't solve the problem of loneliness. Married or not, Christ is the only consistent companion. He is the only One who will always accept you and see your inner beauty. He recognizes your value because He is the One who validated you: He made you and He loves you. You are a child of God, the Creator of heaven and earth.

If you want a new last name, call yourself Godchild. I am Karia Banks Bunting Godchild. What is your name? Every day for the next month, look in the mirror and say, "I am _____ God's child." God has given you a new last name. Your identity is in Christ.

Paul described himself in this way, *"I have been crucified with Christ; and it is no longer I who live, but Christ lives in me"* (Galatians 2:20). As a fellow believer, you too have been crucified with Christ. You arose from the dead with Him. You are seated at the right hand of the Father with Him. You are blessed with all spiritual blessings in the heavenly places with Him. That is how you have the power to live the life God has called you to live.

So, say your name, and put "Godchild" at the end of it because that's who you are. You don't need anybody to improve on that name. Be completely satisfied in Him, and He will satisfy you. He is the only One whose arms will always be open to you. Christ's love is the only consistent love. He is the Friend that never leaves you. To understand and accept this truth is freedom through Christ Jesus. The question is, "What is He asking you to do?"

ALL THAT GLITTERS AIN'T GOLD

I used to tell my daughters, "Everybody is ugly when they get old." I know that is a little crass, I must admit. But it is true. Apart from cosmetic surgery, we wrinkle up, get the turkey sag under the chin, and develop smile lines. My point to them is, look for someone with more than good looks. Have they always listened? No. Have they regretted dating someone based on looks and charm? Absolutely.

Many charming men have been married two and three times. That's how they got married two or three times! The Bible says something about what to look for in a mate in the book of Genesis, chapter 2. Read on to find out what God says.

AN INTIMATE RELATIONSHIP WITH GOD

Scripture reveals how the relationship between God and His creation began: *"Then the Lord God formed man of dust from the ground, and breathed into his nostrils the breath of life; and man became a living being"* (Genesis 2:7).

God named the man Adam. When Adam woke up, he saw God's face. He walked and talked with God. He shared in a divine relationship and received instructions from his Creator. God planned an unprecedented destiny for Adam. Yes, later he made a critical mistake. But even then, because of his preexisting relationship with God, Adam was not destroyed. God spared his life.

When a woman joins her life with a man, a new relationship is born in which she immediately shares his destiny. Because God created the man first, He intended for him to be the leader. The woman is to be his partner who helps him lead. Her position is clearly outlined in Ephesians 5:22, *"Wives, be subject to your own husbands, as to the Lord."* What that means for you is that you must be extremely careful when you decide to be in a marital relationship. You are subject to the authority of your husband, and Scripture commands you to follow him.

If he is a godly man who acknowledges God as his head, you have chosen well. But if you hook up with someone unsavory and he is leading you into a ditch, you are going into the ditch. This principle was established in the words God spoke over Eve, *"Your desire will be for your husband, and he will rule over you"* (Genesis 3:16). Your husband has the opportunity to love you, bless you, and help you to develop. But the reverse is also true because at the same time he has the potential to make you miserable.

Both outcomes depend on his intimacy level with God. If he doesn't work and pay the bills, your credit will be messed up right along with his. But if he works and saves, both of you will be blessed financially. If he has an anger and abuse problem, your well-being and self-esteem will be under attack. If he walks in God's love and peace, you will enjoy coming home to a secure and loving environment.

Furthermore, if he doesn't have an intimate relationship with God, he will guide his own decisions. And Scripture says that the wisdom of a jealous, selfish, arrogant man is demonic (see James 3:15). If he doesn't acknowledge the wisdom of God, what is going to influence his decisions? Demonic wisdom. The atmosphere surrounding such a marriage will be adverse to God and welcoming to the devil.

On the other hand, if a man has wisdom from God, your destiny will be blessed, *"He will be like a tree firmly planted by streams of water, which yields its fruit in its season and its leaf does not wither; and in whatever he does, he prospers"* (Psalm 1:3). During the process of dating or a courtship, you should be able to determine what his relationship with God is. Before you are married if he is attempting to get you to engage in physical intimacy with him, that is a telltale sign. His focus is on self-gratification, and there is very little relationship with God involved.

Now if he is really struggling to restrain his sexual desires, that's another issue. He needs the help of some godly men. But if he doesn't care and doesn't want you to, either—there's a God problem. Then let's say that you do get married, do you really think he's going to quit making decisions based on what he wants at the moment, in spite of what God would have him do? It would greatly benefit you to seriously think about it. His intimacy level with God will determine your future.

RESOURCES FROM ABOVE

"The Lord God planted a garden toward the east, in Eden; and there He placed the man whom He had formed." (Genesis 2:8)

From the time Adam was created, God and Adam had a divinely intimate relationship going on. God was Adam's source, and He supplied all that Adam needed, including a beautiful home. Note in this verse that the Lord God planted the Garden. God even provided the resources to take care of a wife before He gave him a wife.

Ladies, if "home-boy" needs to move in with you, there's a problem. You are not supposed to be the leader, he is. If he is asking you to pay for meals because he doesn't have any money, that's a problem too. He shouldn't even mention that he wants you to help pay his bills because he is in a "tough spot" right now. If he doesn't have a vehicle, and you have to loan him the car that you are paying for so he can take you to and pick you up from work, that's backward.

I don't care if he does keep your car clean. You can go to the car wash and do that yourself. That's not so special. These are all red flag indicators that he is not ready for a relationship with you. Put it on pause and tell him that he needs time to let God provide for his needs. You don't have to date him and pay him, too.

JOB RESPONSIBILITIES

"The Lord God took the man and put him into the garden of Eden to cultivate it and keep it." (Genesis 2:15)

That was a big Garden! Every tree in the Garden was pleasant to the sight and good for food. There was also a river in the Garden that split into four river heads. But God had a plan. Before He gave Adam a wife, God gave him the task of tending the Garden—and there was a lot of work to do. Adam had a job.

Ladies, a man needs to work. He needs something productive to do. God made it a part of his DNA. Even if he has a trust fund set up in his name, is independently wealthy, or is happily and securely retired, he needs to do something productive. If he is doing nothing either because he has so much money that he doesn't need to work, or because he is too lazy to work, both situations will cause you much grief. No matter how good he looks, how much potential he has, how large his estate is, or how much gold he has on his wrist, fingers, or teeth; even if he has a heart of gold—he still needs a job.

LOOKING FOR MR. RIGHT

Some men don't want to get married. Therefore, they don't need to get married. If you are dating someone and he really doesn't want to marry, leave him alone. If a man wants to marry you, he will make it known to you. But if it's taking him ten years to make up his mind, he doesn't really want to marry you. He might settle for you because you have great attributes. You have been a faithful friend throughout the years. He knows you like the back of his hand, and you know him that way. You both know each other's likes and dislikes. It seems as though it could work.

But if you have to push him to tie the knot, he really doesn't want to do it. Who needs a situation like that? You don't want to end up in a marriage where he feels trapped. He will resent you for it. You want to be loved; you deserve to be loved. God loves you, and if you are going to get married, wait until He gives you someone who really loves you.

God is so wise. Prior to giving Adam a wife, He allowed Adam to experience what it's like to be alone. Adam needed to know that no matter how hard he looked, he could not find a helper suitable for him. Then when God brought Adam his wife, he appreciated her. Let God present you to your husband. Let Him present you to a mate who has experienced his own need and who is ready to love you with his whole heart.

DIVORCED NOT DEJECTED

Sometimes people marry for all the wrong reasons, only to find that it just won't work out. Sometimes people marry with all of the right intentions, and the marriage still doesn't survive. God never intended divorce, and you didn't either. You tried to avoid the disappointment, the pain, the heartbreaking end. Divorce can leave a person's life in shambles. It can cause a woman to have concerns and fears about her future.

But you have to remember that God still loves you, and He will always take care of you. God wants you to know how valuable you are to Him. In His own words, Jesus explained why we should not be afraid, *"Are not two sparrows sold for a cent? And yet not one of them will fall to the ground apart from your Father. But the very hairs of your head are all numbered. So do not fear; you are more valuable than many sparrows"* (Matthew 10:29–31).

All of nature, including the birds of the air, experiences God's protection. His creatures—big and small—do not have to worry about what will happen to them. If you are feeling insecure, unprotected, unsure, and have serious questions about your future, you should know that God has provided everything that you need to cope with your situation. Scripture promises that *"God hath not given us the spirit of fear; but of power, and of love, and of a sound mind"* (2 Timothy 1:7 KJV). When you are confident that God loves you, His reassuring words can make all the difference for you. In the midst of your troubles, you only need to trust Him.

Ladies, you do not have to be afraid of your future; that is not of God. He has given you the power that you need to prepare for it and make all the adjustments you are required to make. He has given you the ability to love so that you will hold no bitterness against anyone. Bitterness and a lack of forgiveness will only cause harm to you— your ex-husband will go on with his life. If you continue to harbor resentment in your heart, it will affect your overall judgment and be detrimental to your well-being.

Yet there are legitimate concerns, and there seems to be so much to be afraid of. You don't have the money that you used to have, and it doesn't seem fair. No matter which way you slice it, two incomes were better than one. Maybe you didn't have to earn an income before the divorce. Now you are feeling the stress of having to fight him for child support.

At the same time, you need to earn a living to take care of your-self and your family's needs. Because of the hours that you work, you can't watch the children as closely, and you have to rely on others to be there for you. It is hard not to worry about what will happen to you and them. Although you are tired when you get home, you're grate-ful for your job because it takes your mind off of your personal wor-ries. At least there you can have peace for a few hours.

Moreover, you didn't think about it so much before but now you're concerned about crime. When there was a man in the house, at least he would defend your family against an intruder. Now, who would help if someone broke in? Surely they could overpower you. You realize you need an alarm system or extra door locks. You have to be more careful, but you can't let your fear show. You pray that no one will pay atten-tion to the fact that it is just you and the kids alone in your house.

You're also anxious about your health. If something happens to you, then what will happen to the children? If you get sick, who will take care of you? All of these issues can cause a woman to fear. Fear preys on the mind, and once it takes hold, it feeds itself and contin-ues to grow. That is why God equips you to maintain the soundness of your mind so that you can keep your priorities straight. He does-n't want worry to be your priority; He wants you to depend on His faithfulness to watch over all of your cares.

The *New American Standard Bible* (NASB) uses the term "disci-pline" to describe what having a sound mind means. God has empow-ered you to use self-control as you put the pieces of your life together and move into your future destiny. It is the Lord's desire for you to be whole in your spirit, soul, and body—that is how He designed you.

There are immense benefits to be gained in trusting God to ful-fill His promises. He will never let you down. I like the way that God described Himself to His servant Abram. This man believed God against all odds. Although Abram was human and may have showed signs of weakness during his time of waiting on God, his faith in God's promises did not waver. God told him, *"I am a shield to you; your reward shall be very great"* (Genesis 15:1).

In order to come through a divorce without being damaged and dejected, God must be your shield and your reward. In other words, He must be your focus. You may have poured your life into your marriage, thinking a good marriage would be your reward. It didn't work out. But God is still with you. He wants you to be secure and satisfied with Him.

It's so crucial to follow God's counsel. The Word says to *"set your mind on things above, not on the things that are on earth"* (Colossians 3:2). If you do what God says, you can escape mental captivity. Keeping your focus on Him will free you from having to worry about your survival. You will endure to the end because He loves you and He will instruct you in the best way to pursue goal-oriented living. With God's help, you are not a victim—you are a victor.

But what if you say, "I am so depressed. What if I can't even get out of bed?" Don't allow depression to assume authority over your disposition. Maybe it's time to seek the help of a Christian counselor, someone who will guide you to God's answer for your situation. It would be good if you take some time and examine your heart. Find some quiet time and spend it with God. The Holy Spirit will help you see that you don't have to accept fear, regret, guilt, shame, pain, insecurity, and a sense of inferiority. These are the emotions keeping you in the bed; they can lure you into thinking that it helps you to avoid the pain.

Fear is of the devil. Allow the Word of God to overcome it. God has given you victory; get up! You will heal. Take it one step at a time and put one foot in front of the other—just keep going. It may take a little time, but eventually you'll walk right out of the mess. No matter how unsuccessful you think you've been so far, your future is not equal to your past. If you keep feeding your faith with God's Word, you will reap the benefits of your efforts. God will see your faith and reward you. Keep trying.

Choose not to give up when things get tough. I cannot stress enough how imperative it is to seek a fresh relationship with God and trust in Him, and not in yourself. He will give you His joy, and that will be your strength. Wait on the Lord to deliver you, knowing that

He will. Although it feels like you've been knocked down, and you're wondering if you will ever recover—it's really a test of your faith.

Do you believe God will come through for you? He will, because He loves you. Get up out of that bed. Do something. Go to a women's Bible study. Surround yourself with women of faith. Don't faint now. Your future will be more wonderful than your past. Get up!

Some of you are not in a physical bed. You are lying in the bed of self-pity and regret. You wish you hadn't, you wish he hadn't; you just wish. Quit looking in the rearview mirror of your life. You can't change the past, but you can look forward to the future. Rest in the truth that God loves you and that He is in control. He wants to give you a glorious future if you trust Him. You, too, must get up!

CHRIST'S WIDOW IN A SEXY WORLD

In his single set of instructions, Paul also addressed his message of godly conduct to widows, *But I say to the unmarried and to widows that it is good for them if they remain even as I. But if they do not have self-control, let them marry; for it is better to marry than to burn with passion"* (1 Corinthians 7:8–9).

In the wee hours of the morning, you lie in bed with a tearstained face, and there is no one there to comfort you. Your being aches to hear his voice, but your yearnings will remain unsatisfied. He is not there; he has gone home to be with the Lord.

Your emotions are all over the place. One minute you are panic-stricken and the next you are full of faith. Your feelings fluctuate between confusion, exhaustion, and sorrow. At times you feel abandoned, at other times you are joyful. You battle with discouragement and hope. The two of you were together for so long, and now he is gone. *How dare he!* you think. But you know that he would want you to keep living. And so it is as you walk in God's grace.

Your husband made you feel like you belonged to someone. In many ways, your identity was his. When someone said your name, it was joined by the conjunction "and," then his name. All of a sudden, there is no one there to represent that name, and there is a void that makes you now feel like only one-half of your previous identity. Sometimes people act as if you have a disease that they might catch. They don't know what to say and cut conversations short because they're uncomfortable talking with you. There are times when you feel empty and purposeless.

The Lord's heart is with widows. If you are a widow, He loves you, He sees you, and He will look after you. God defends you from those who would harm you. He judges people based on how they treat you. He will come to your aid when you call Him. The psalmist David spoke of God's protective covering over you, describing God as *"a father of the fatherless and a judge for the widows, is God in His holy habitation"* (Psalm 68:5). God will punish anyone who takes advantage of widows in an unfortunate situation. Those who accept a widow's offering will be judged by whether they knowingly took what she needed for her own subsistence.

On the other hand, when people show genuine concern and come by to visit you, they are doing God's bidding. When social organizations stand up for the rights of the underprivileged, they are doing God's will. When ministries provide for a widow's needs and offer a level of comfort and support, they are obeying Scripture. God has not left you alone.

But I also have to warn you, as much as God loves you, He also has expectations about how you will conduct yourself. His Word helps us understand the role of the church, *"Honor widows who are widows indeed; but if any widow has children or grandchildren, they must first learn to practice piety in regard to their own family and to make some return to their parents; for this is acceptable in the sight of God. Now she who is a widow indeed and who has been left alone, has fixed her hope on God and continues in entreaties and prayers night and day. But she who gives herself to wanton pleasure is dead even while she lives"* (1 Timothy 5:3–6).

In this passage, Paul wrote to Timothy, his beloved son in the ministry, instructing him how to care for the widows in the congregation.

In doing so, he established the order for how churches are to conduct their ministry to this beloved segment of God's family. According to Scripture, if you are a widow, you are eligible to receive help if you are really in need. However, if you have family, they have the primary responsibility for taking care of you.

But if you have no family and are really alone, the Lord wants you to do three specific things. You must ask yourself the following questions. How you respond to them will determine whether you are in agreement with God's will for you: (1) Do you put your hope in God? (2) Do you pray night and day? (3) Are you asking God for help?

1. Are you hoping in God for your welfare? It is possible to be a widow who has hope in someone or something other than God. If you are not hoping in God, your focus is on worldly affairs. This means you are looking for comfort, companionship, and financial resources outside of what God offers you. You might be looking to friends or a recently acquired companion to provide for you. In that case, you should not look to the church for support. Ask those in whom you hope.

2. Do you pray night and day? This question reveals not only how close you are to God, but what you are doing on behalf of other people. I have great admiration for an older woman of God whom I love dearly. She is in her 90's now and her ministry is prayer. She keeps a prayer journal and literally prays night and day that God will provide for other people.

   My own father is deceased, and my mother has Alzheimer's disease. I was recently taking a walk and feeling sorry for myself. I complained to the Lord, "Who will pray for me now? How in the world will I be successful at anything I do without a prayer covering?" Then the Lord rebuked me and brought this lovely woman to my mind. I realize now that she is my prayer covering. How I value her! I know that when I'm busy or distracted, somebody is still praying. She wages war in prayer.

She is a benefit to the kingdom of God and freely gives what she has to offer. This woman is doing what God expects of her as a widow who is pursuing God's heart.

3. Are you asking God to help you? Is He the focus of your life, or are you and your friends the focus of your life? You are eligible for help from the church if God is your everything, and you are sold out to Him.

   On the other hand, God says don't double-dip. He wants you to live for Him and not for pleasure alone. Don't try to get your pleasure from the world and expect the church to treat you like a widow. That is not fair to the women who really need the church's help.

   Some people are glad to be widowed. If a woman's husband was sick for some time, it was a lot of work taking care of him all those years. She was faithful when he was alive. But he's been dead for a while, and it is time for her to start living! And live she does. All that pent-up frustration is released in evenings of dancing, partying, and maybe even a little drinking. If you are living it up in a grand social life, doing whatever you want to do, the Word of God says you are dead, even while you live.

   Furthermore, if you are a younger widow, Paul says you may need to get married again. He is referring to you "thirty-somethings." Maybe your husband died and left you money. Your temptation is to live well; you have the ability to travel, shop, visit friends, and do little else. You become a coast-to-coast gossip and a busybody, telling people in California what is going on in Texas, and people in Texas what is going on in California.

   You know all the news because you have so much time on your hands to find out. People like going places with you because you are fun to be with! But since you have nothing else to do, you tell it all to anyone who will listen. You were created for productivity, so Paul says it is best for you to have a new hus-band and the responsibilities of a family.

If you agree with that suggestion, then follow God's direc-tion. Until then, the same set of instructions that Paul gives to the unmarried applies to you. God gives a single set of instruc-tions.

A word of caution for the mature woman with a lot of assets who may be looking to remarry: First of all make sure that the man you are dating is not a gold digger. What is his repu-tation? Listen to what wise and spiritual people say in spite of how you feel. As a widowed woman, if you want to make sure the work that you and your husband engaged in prior to his death stays with your children; think about putting your assets in a trust. Do some estate planning to work out all the details. Then, if God and your spiritual mentors agree—get married!

WALKING IN YOUR DIVINE DESIGN

When you attend an exercise class, at the end of a session, the instructor will often say, "Walk it out." What they want you to do is walk around and shake your legs so that your muscles don't get tight. They want you to keep moving.

God wants you to keep moving too. The cross of Calvary made a way for you to become a child of God. That is your identity. Focus on your identity in Him and move forward. As you walk, know that God is the answer you have been seeking. He is your constant companion; and without Him we can do nothing. As Scripture says to us, *"In Him we live and move and exist . . . 'For we also are His children'"* (Acts 17:28). He is able to take care of you, love you, protect you, enable you, and complete you. Trust Him with the life that He has entrusted to you.

Till Death Do You Part: *Living Happy and Married*

*J*okes about the subject of marriage abound. I came across some cute ones recently. Here are a few of my favorites that I found in the book *777 Great Clean Jokes*.[10] In one story, a father and his little son were talking. The father was showing his son some pictures from the day that he and his wife were married. The little one was smiling and pointing, enjoying the attention of his father. Suddenly, a thought popped into his brain. The boy looked at his father and raised a curious eyebrow. "Daddy," he asked, "is this when Mommy came to work for us?"

Definitely rings a bell. Or, how about this one: A man and his wife attended a dinner party at their friend's home. Near the end of the meal, the wife reprimanded her husband. "That's the third time you've gone for dessert," she scolded. "Our hostess must think that you're an absolute pig." He replied, "I don't think so. I've been telling her that it's for you."

I especially like the joke about the wedding anniversary. One morning, a woman said to her husband, "I bet you don't know what day this is." Going out the door on his way to the office, he responded indignantly, "Of course, I do." At 11:00 a.m., the doorbell rang. When the woman answered it, she was handed a box containing a dozen long-stemmed red roses. At 1:00 p.m., a foil-wrapped box of her favorite chocolates arrived. Later in the afternoon, an exclusive boutique delivered a designer dress.

The woman couldn't wait for her husband to come home. "First the flowers, then the candy, and then the dress!" she exclaimed when he walked in the door. "I've never had a more wonderful Groundhog Day in my whole life!"

I should try that sometimes and see if it works! Some marriage jokes are only funny because they reveal a strange, but common, perspective. Take this one for example: Attending a wedding ceremony for the first time, a little girl whispered to her mother, "Why is the bride all dressed in white?" Her mother explained, "Because white is the color of happiness." She continued, "And today is the happiest day of her life." The child thought for a moment and then asked, "So why is the groom wearing black?"

The truth is, there are a lot of married people who wedded with dreams of a bright future in their eyes only to have found their marriages shrouded in black. What on earth could have possibly happened?

Marriage involves two people. If it didn't, each individual could rule their territory from the throne of their own perspectives, demanding the edicts of their own desires. But there is a problem with that approach—that's not being married. That is called being single. And, unfortunately, there are a lot of married people trying to live as though they're single. They have a separate bank account, make their own decisions, pick up their own dinner on the way home from the office and eat it by themselves, enjoy recreation separately, and watch different television programs in different rooms. They live in separate worlds and pray apart, go to church apart, and have different friends.

Then they wonder, "What's wrong with my marriage?" Being

married is both an art and a science. The science of marriage is revealed in saying "I do" in front of him at the altar. That is to be followed up by daily saying "I do" in response to the principles of Christ in your relationship. But marriage is also an art because two spirits must find a way to become one. It is the art of getting to know the person to whom you are married and learning to move in syncopation with him.

It is the art of reading each other's eyes and feeling each other's heart. It is the art of anticipating what the other would think when he or she is not around, and acting accordingly. It is the art of loving him even when he doesn't seem to love you back or serving her when she doesn't act like she needs you. It is the art of a warrior love that must learn to act selflessly so that the marriage will survive.

BECOMING HIS PLAYMATE

Would you believe that Hugh Hefner has something right? His methods are carnal and devious. His message is profane. His life and influence is a testimony to the deception of demonic forces. But, believe it or not, his premise that man needs a playmate is actually biblical.

Many of us have heard the axiom "All work and no play makes Johnny a dull boy." All work and no play will not only make Johnny a dull boy, it makes Mary an unbiblical wife. The reason for this is found in Genesis 2:18 where God stated His purpose for the creation of woman. God said, *"It is not good for the man to be alone; I will make him a helper suitable for him."* The first part is clear: *"It is not good for man to be alone."* Yet, many of us are guilty of leaving our husbands alone far too much. We think that they don't need us to play and have fun.

As a result, we hardly ever give a thought to participating in fun things with him. But at the same time, we insist that we both share the tasks of managing the household, making sure dinner is prepared, caring for the children, and paying the bills. This means that we have only a partial understanding of our role as a wife that doesn't go far enough. Many of us consider it our responsibility to maximize our earning potential and contribute to the family's finances. We accept the fact that we

need to volunteer at our children's schools. But the thought that our husbands need a playmate is frequently the furthest thing from our mind.

Every once in a while, you need to pause and remember the time
when you were dating. You enjoyed going to football games and movies
together. You'd even be willing to go fishing with him sometimes, and
he just might attend the symphony with you. On the weekends, you
looked for adventuresome trips like driving to an arts festival in the
neighboring town. Hand in hand, you walked through the crowded
streets of the State Fair, eating funnel cakes and turkey legs, listening
to the sweet music of the merry-go-round, and hearing the distant
shrieks of the bungee jumpers who didn't realize jumping would be
that scary!

But how many of us can identify with this scenario? At a certain
stage, you've become plain boring, and he is too. If you are working
late, he's watching TV, hanging out with his friends, playing golf, or
bowling. On the days when you are off, he has other things to do. You
have meetings, work, soccer games, and lessons to take the kids to on
Saturdays. He has the yard work to do, and after that he's got some
errands he has to run.

Honestly, you didn't want to run with him anyway, even if the kids
didn't have practice. You're a little perturbed because the carpet needs
to be shampooed, he hasn't fixed the toilet or called somebody to fix
it, and the light bulb is out in the laundry room. Do you have to do
everything? Before you know it, Saturday has come and gone, and
you're looking at each other with jaded eyes. All you have left to offer
each other is the last traces of your energy. Not a thought has been
given to sincere, intense playtime. No playing. No playmate.

On the other hand, maybe you're a woman who strives to be a
genuine partner in every way with her husband. You set joint agendas
for what you need to accomplish and follow those agendas. You participate in the same civic organizations or join complementary organizations so that the family's influence is multiplied. You make money
together, and you budget your money together.

However, even with all of this going for you, for some reason your marriage doesn't seem quite right at times. And you can't figure out why. You begin to think, *What's going on? We're not clicking.* Check your playmate status. Working through life together can be fraught with challenges and conflict. You think things should go one way, and he thinks things should go another way. It's not always easy to reach a compromise.

Maybe the start-up company was your idea, but you decided to go with his judgment on a major decision and it didn't work out. Maybe you made a decision with which he disagreed, and it has caused problems. Maybe your job carries a great deal of responsibility and you travel extensively. Or perhaps your work schedule is exactly the opposite of your mate's.

The daily stress of trying to hold it together has produced an emotional crisis. The children sense the tension and have become rebellious. Because of that development, you and your husband are blaming each other. You wish that he would communicate more, and he would just like to be left alone.

Playtime won't solve everything, but it could open up communication. Take some time for rest and relaxation; then, over dinner and a movie, you might discover the issues that need to be addressed. Along the way, you might enjoy yourself and rediscover the man you married! Find ways to be his playmate. That's your responsibility.

My husband and I have set aside a date night for twenty-four years. It is wonderful. Whether we have money or we're flat broke, we do something together every other Friday night. I remember one of those evenings when we really didn't have any money. We went to a local restaurant and ordered an appetizer—buffalo chicken wings, I think it was. Then we took our little wings to the parking lot of the dollar movie, ate them, and laughed about how broke we were. After our scrumptious meal, we gathered our pennies, bought our dollar movie tickets, and took a seat on the back row where we could cuddle and laugh unnoticed.

It amazes me how, over the years, we have met so many couples that have not gone out together since before their children were born.

The idea of going to a movie or a concert together is nonexistent. We love to hook up with other couples and enjoy watching as they take the journey toward reintroducing the fun of playtime into their relationships.

You might say, "My husband doesn't want a playmate." Sure, he does. He plays with somebody, doesn't he? Just see if that person can be you sometime. You might have to be a little assertive and ask for the date night. Perhaps you need to take the initiative and arrange the babysitter, if that's necessary. You may have to endure a few quiet car rides. If the two of you are a little rusty when it comes to being alone, there's no guarantee that you won't get your feelings hurt a couple of times. This may be an area of growth for you and your husband, but you can't grow what you don't plant. Pray and ask for God to give you the grace and then begin the process of being a playmate.

THAT SMILE

During my unmarried days, I remember coming home one summer from college. I have always been a carefree and easygoing person. But that year had been particularly difficult. My grades hadn't been so good, and I had college-related relationship issues. (Many of you know what I mean!) That summer, although I didn't have a car, I got a full-time job with an insurance company on the other side of town. I attended the local university at night.

Although my parents had five cars, I was an independent young lady. I was going to do this on my own. So I would get up really early in the morning and catch the bus to work. Then I would work my eight-hour shift, walk to the local bus stop, and catch the bus to the university. I got out of class every night at 9:30 p.m. and made my way home. I would usually get in around 10:30 p.m. Then, I studied. The next morning, I'd get up and repeat the process.

One morning, my dad saw me dragging myself to the bathroom to get ready for work. He looked at me and said, "Life will wipe that smile off your face, won't it?" Strangely enough, that was a word of comfort to me. I just looked at him and nodded my head.

For some of you, life has wiped the smile off your face. You no longer look at your husband, or life, with that gleam of joy and promise in your eyes. You aren't a playmate because you don't feel like playing. You are tired, you are hurt, the kids are noisy, and you just want some time alone.

Prayer is the key to balancing your busy life. Get up early enough to talk with the Lord. Praying can be viewed as a paradox. It seems like it takes time, but it actually gives it. Ask God how you should order your day. Let Him schedule the items on your daytimer. Let Him inform you of what is important and what is not. Let Him prepare you for what lies ahead. Many times you are stressed and tired because you are doing what doesn't need to be done, worrying about what hasn't been done, and not doing the things that should be done.

Then again, sometimes you're emotionally drained because you don't know what will happen to you. And you don't know if you can handle your feelings of despair. You're working so hard and have become weary because you don't seem to be getting where you are trying to go. In fact, the conflict between work and home is wearing you out. You're disappointed because you can't get the help that you are too tired to ask for. Furthermore, nobody seems to appreciate all that you do.

Well, hold on. Wait a minute. Tell Jesus about it. Unload your worries. Minute by minute, hour by hour, unload. Listen for His Spirit to direct you and redirect you. Maybe you don't need to be the mom who drives the kids to the game. Maybe you don't really have to go in to the office this Saturday. Maybe somebody else can bring the treats this time. Maybe you don't need to go tonight—you need a good episode of your favorite program and a pint of ice cream.

When was the last time you and your husband stayed at a hotel and slept in? The Holy Spirit knows what you need, and He will prompt your heart when you take the time to listen and communicate with Him in prayer. Go ahead. Make His day.

There is a wonderful Scripture that is very encouraging to those who may have become discouraged while pursuing their goals, it says, *"Delight yourself in the Lord; and He will give you the desires of your heart. Commit your way to the Lord, trust also in Him; and He will do it"* (Psalm 37:4–5). When you find pleasure in serving the Lord, He places God-inspired desires within you. God is so perfect in His plan that the thing that He gives you and the thing that you desire are one and the same.

God gives you talents, or gifts, that you don't have to strive, cry, or strain to achieve. Certain things come easy to you. For example, some people can sing, and everyone who hears them says that they have the voice of an angel. It just comes naturally for them and they enjoy singing. That is an ability that God has placed inside them and they honor God when they use it. It pleases Him when we exercise His gifts to glorify Him. The more we find ways to use the gifts God gives us, the more we find delight in Him. It is a mutually satisfying exchange.

We all have at least one special gift from God in which we excel. So don't worry; you don't have to be grouchy about it and insult other people. You don't have to be irritable and impatient or promote yourself. You don't have to be unethical, compromise your values, or abandon your home. God will fulfill the desires that He gives you at the right time.

That is such a relief because all you have to do to make it happen is be willing to use your gift and God will take care of your success. The burden for you to reach your destiny is not on your shoulders. God will bring it to pass. As you spend time with Him, God will put the sparkle back in your eyes and the hope back into your heart.

When you connect with God in prayer, and commit to being a playmate to your husband, God will smile on you. Allow Him to adjust your priorities and refocus your attention to line up with His desires for your life. You will be more fulfilled than you could ever imagine, and you'll be functioning according to your divine design. Trust God. He is faithful.

DIFFERENT AS NIGHT AND DAY

So you complain because your husband's ways are different than yours? Well, he's supposed to be different. It's all right for one of you to be messy and the other a neat-freak. It's really okay for you to be outgoing while he's introverted and reserved. He might be a workaholic and you're laid back—no problem. You know the old adage: opposites attract. There is a lot of truth in that statement. The key ingredient in a marriage is striking the right balance between the two partners.

We can find the description of a godly husband and wife in the Bible. Not only did God design the two of you, He also designed the institution of marriage. So, common sense says we have to consult the Master Designer to find out what He has to say about how we must conduct ourselves and our marriages.

Think about it. If both you and your husband were the same, neither one of you could help the other. Neither one of you could balance the checkbook, and both of you would be neat-freaks who liked things a particular way. There would be nobody that could keep the other from working all the time; or, for that matter, playing all the time. All the money would be gone because either one of you could have spent it. If guests came over they would fall through the couch because neither of you would take the responsibility to replace the furniture.

When you think about your husband, think like the biblical character Job who asked, *"Did not He who made me in the womb make him, and the same one fashion us in the womb?"* (Job 31:15). Just like you, your husband is *"fearfully and wonderfully made"* (Psalm 139:14). It is pride that produces the perception that others are inadequate.

The Word of God responds to people who get impatient with each other in this way: *"Do not complain, brethren, against one another, so that you yourselves may not be judged; behold, the Judge is standing right at the door"* (James 5:9). The act of complaining carries the idea of groaning, grumbling, or uttering a deep sigh. In other words, don't get exasperated with your husband and exaggerate your dissatisfaction to the extent that you become vocal about your displeasure. God says that you'll be judged for it!

From the beginning, the man and the woman were created to be different. The book of Genesis is clear on that. Man was made out of dirt, and woman was made out of bone. Both are enduring substances. When ancient tombs are opened, archaeologists find dirt and bone. Bones do not disintegrate, and dirt doesn't disappear. God made man and woman out of enduring materials. Both are strong, and both serve their own purpose.

ME, TARZAN; YOU, JANE

After man was created, he was placed in the Garden by himself, in the middle of all the trees, rivers, and animals. He was the first Tarzan. I can just see him swinging from tree to tree; after all, that was a lot of ground to cover! The woman, on the other hand, was built by God and escorted to the man. She was his Jane. She was never by herself and never exposed to the elements without having someone beside her.

The man was excited when God brought her to him. He knew where she had come from: the wound in his side was still fresh. He was her protector. She was divinely connected to him.

In the book of Isaiah, the lack of availability of husbands as a source of protection and blessing was the result of a curse on the land. The prophet Isaiah wrote about the judgment to be executed on Israel: *"For seven women will take hold of one man in that day, saying, 'We will eat our own bread and wear our own clothes, only let us be called by your name; take away our reproach!'"* (Isaiah 4:1). Whether you are married or not—you need a protector—a covering. And that covering needs to have God's authority to function in that capacity. The three areas where God invests the authority to shepherd people are: parents, husbands, and pastors. Whichever is appropriate for you, allow one of them to serve as the protective function in your life.

When God created woman, not only did He say that it was not good for man to be alone, but also that He would make a helper suitable for him (see Genesis 2:18). The Hebrew word for help-meet is *ezer*; it is used to describe those who serve as a helper to another. The word also refers to what the Holy Spirit does for believers in His role as a companion and a comforter. This same word is referred to in Exodus 18:4: *"The other was named Eliezer; for he said, 'the God of my father, was my help, and delivered me from the sword of Pharaoh.'"* The word is used again in Psalm 10:14, which reads, *"You have been the helper of the orphan."*

The term "helper" never carries the idea of inferiority; rather, the idea of lending one's strength to another so that they are successful. Have you ever heard the phrase spoken of a mother, "She's the backbone of the family"? Or have you heard it said of a woman with a successful husband, "She's the reason he is so successful"? These are women who perform their *ezer* responsibilities! Because of her role, a woman is not only created to be connected and protected—she is also created to be respected!

Perhaps today you have a headache, and your husband's "yelling and swinging through the trees" is the source of it. You are in need of prayer because your husband has traits that aggravate you. Yet they are in line with his design. Maybe you want to be more connected with him, and he's always too busy playing Tarzan. Sister, it is part of his makeup to swing through the trees. Let him swing. But don't forget, he really does need you. It would most likely be his great delight for you to comment on how suave and exceptional his swing is.

There may be times that you are focused on him when his focus is somewhere else. Don't be upset, that's part of his design. Sometimes it is the reverse and he needs your attention. God may have made you the go-getter in the family. In your opinion, he is entirely too laid back. Make sure you don't take over his role in the family—that will emasculate him. He will only rebel in either overt or passive-aggressive ways.

After all, he wants to be the one swinging through the trees and protecting you from the wild animals. If you, strong woman, don't need for him to do that, what exactly is he going to do? You may be very capable, but he is your marriage partner for a reason.

Remember, it is about balance between the two of you. He has qualities you lack, and you have qualities that he lacks. Scripture says in Proverbs 14:1, *"The wise woman builds her house, but the foolish tears it down with her own hands."* Be strong, but be sensitive. Because we have *ezer* capabilities, many women selfishly use that ability for ourselves and scorn the attempts of our husbands to assert themselves. When we do that, we demonstrate that we really don't understand the purpose of our gifting.

There may be times when your husband is weak; particularly if he doesn't have a job, recently retired, wasted away some money, or lost a business. Then, *ezer*, it's time to bear up under the stress that circumstance puts on the family. Proverbs 24:10 has a strong warning, *"If you are slack in the day of distress, your strength is limited."*

But do not despair. God created the woman after He had put man in a deep sleep; He alone knows how woman was created, but man doesn't. Man not only did not have anything to do with it, he wasn't even awake! God intended it to be that way, because He was the one who caused Adam to fall into a deep sleep. My point is, your husband doesn't know you inside and out in the same way that God does.

God knows you, God made you, God accepts you, and God loves you—just like you are. That means that you don't have to be afraid of rejection, because the God who loves you will not reject you. He may improve you, but He doesn't dismiss you. He doesn't dislike you just because you fail. He doesn't evaluate you and decide you are inadequate just because you feel inadequate.

You can rest in His love when you get it right and when you get it wrong. He forgives you when you fail and admit it, throwing your sin as far from Him as the east is from the west. He's always working in you to make you more like Him—on your good days and bad days. When you bring your problems to Him and talk to Him, He keeps your thinking straight. He's patient. He never gives up and never gives up on you. He's your chief, number one advocate—even when He's your only advocate. He delights in your achievements, and encourages you when you are discouraged.

He sees inside of you and knows how you feel; He understands why you do what you do. His judgments are always righteous. Because He knows you, He never misunderstands or misjudges your motives. He doesn't have any faults, so He doesn't have any personal faults that He needs to attribute to you. He doesn't agree with what people say about you when they are wrong. Yet, He doesn't excuse your behavior; He holds you accountable. But He does it with love and grace. He hugs you, even while He is disciplining you. His heart smiles at you.

A classic hymn, "Love Divine, All Loves Excelling," by Charles Wesley, that speaks to my spirit says, "Love divine, all loves excelling, joy of heaven, to earth come down; fix in us thy humble dwelling; all thy faithful mercies crown! Jesus thou art all compassion, pure, unbounded love thou art; visit us with thy salvation; enter every trembling heart."[11]

On the other hand, having said all of that, your husband isn't God. Don't expect him to be. Don't expect him to never reject you; you'll find yourself disappointed. Don't expect him to always watch out for your best interest over his; sometimes he will, and sometimes he won't. There are things about you that you will have to help him come to understand. He might think that he knows you thoroughly, but he can never know you like God knows you. So his judgments are not always going to be righteous.

Sometimes he will "sleep" though conversations about things of importance to you or be insensitive through difficult moments in your life. Choose not to get angry at him for what you see as his inadequacies. Don't be impatient with him when he is doing something differently than the way you would do it. He is the Lord's servant, and only through the Lord's doing—he is yours.

Provide help for your husband without needing his constant validation. Get your validation from your Creator and serve your husband. There will be times when your husband recognizes how precious you are, but there will be times when he won't. It was the Lord God who took one of Adam's ribs from him and closed up the place with flesh. The Lord God *took* Adam's rib—the man did not volunteer it. He couldn't even identify his need, let alone volunteer to sacrifice a portion of his body to fulfill it. Just as the Lord God caused Adam to sacrifice, it is the Lord God that causes a man, your husband, to sacrifice for you.

Chances are you cannot talk your husband into willingly doing anything for you that he didn't really want to do in the first place. But, Scripture tells us that *"the king's heart is like channels of water in the hand of the Lord; He turns it wherever He wishes"* (Proverbs 21:1). In other words, the head of the family is in the hands of the Lord. We want the head of the household to be obedient to the Lord and submit to His authority alone. It is our job to seek God on behalf of the "king" and intercede for him so that he will be successful in doing his job.

After He had taken the rib, the Lord God also healed Adam's body. To have Eve in his life cost Adam a part of himself. The Lord loved Adam, and the temporary wound was meant to bring closeness to him, rather than distance. Don't be afraid to cost your husband something. If you are a stay-at-home mom and you need an allowance, don't be afraid to ask for it. Whether in the home or at your place of employment, your work has value.

If you like flowers, gifts, or cards, it is not selfish to ask for those things—even if your family is on a tight budget. There is nothing wrong with expecting him to pay the bills and not sit on the couch, play ball, or putter around the garage while you work. There may be times when he will have to sacrifice to fulfill his biblical responsibilities related to you. But after you cost him something—massage his spirit, his soul, and his body. Don't leave him with a gaping hole.

DESIGNED TO DOMINATE

In the beginning, the Lord God commanded, *"And let them rule over the fish of the sea and over the birds of the sky and over the cattle and over all the earth, and over every creeping thing that creeps on the earth"* (Genesis 1:26). Just like your Creator, you are designed to rule, to dominate. In other words, you were made to succeed. God trusts you enough to share responsibility with you.

You are fully empowered and authorized to do what God has called you to do. Your only limitation is you and whether you believe that you can do it. God has gifted you with abilities, which you must develop and offer to God for service. He's turned the earth over to His children and that includes you. He wants you to do a good job ruling it and make Him proud.

However, the power to dominate was not given to the male or female. It was given to both. If you are married, this means that you have a great opportunity to expand your influence. Provided you don't compete against each other, the two of you together can complement each other. When you work together, you can accomplish so much more. The ability to rule requires strategy, thought, and action. It is better for God's people to rule than people who do not have the Spirit of God within them. However, God's people must rule in accordance with His principles and priorities.

When God made the decision to give dominion to the male and female, He was not confused. It was not an accident when He allowed the woman to have the responsibility of dominion along with the man. His decision was not ill-considered. He knew that a woman would have a different function than a man; He created her that way. But when He decided how He wanted His earth to be administrated, He wanted to empower both the man and woman to do the job.

According to your divine design, you were created both to complement and partner with your husband. Exercise your dominion together through planning, hard work, and focus. Follow God and obey His direction. As you partner together, you will make great progress.

ENTERTAINMENT TONIGHT

We have arrived at the subject newlyweds love to talk about: physical intimacy. There is no doubt that God's plan involved physical union between a man and a woman. So if God talked about it, we'll talk about it.

Do you realize that God has a plan for sexual union? The book of Genesis, chapter 2, verse 24 provides the explanation: *"For this reason a man shall leave his father and his mother, and be joined to his wife; and they shall become one flesh."* The first thing to note is that prior to the union of a man and woman, the man should leave his father and his mother. In the Old Testament, parents were two of the most significant people in a young man's life. They held on to the right to be obeyed by their offspring. Furthermore, it was the custom of the day that the parents would actually arrange their children's marriage.

The Bible is clear, though, no matter how strong the bond between parents and children—after the choice to be married was made and the man took his wife—priorities changed. The newlyweds left the old family structure and clung to each other. The principle in this passage is that the man will leave the significant influences in his life and cleave to his wife.

The word "cleave" carries the idea of sticking like glue. As such, a man is commanded to cleave to his wife; he is to stick to his wife like glue. Likewise, she must stick to him. Have you ever seen couples, particularly older ones, who just stick to each other? I have an uncle and aunt like that, my Uncle Tom and Aunt Rose. They have been married for what seems like forever; and if you see one, you see the other. They are a team and take such good care of each other.

Maybe you have someone in your family like this or know of older couples that are still crazy about each other. It is obvious that they belong together; it seems like they share each other's breath. Their love is so evident—not because they are holding hands, but because they are holding each other's lives. That's how God designed the relationship between a husband and his wife: He wants you and your husband to stick together.

The Word of God is not suggesting that there aren't other important relationships in a couple's life. It is pointing out that the main priority should be the relationship between you and your mate. But, sisters, let me caution you, in your role as a wife, you must be careful to maintain a disposition that your husband will desire to "stick" to. Depending on several factors that may affect a woman's disposition, sometimes we can have a disagreeable attitude without really noticing it.

It seems to be a trait of human nature to have a tendency that overlooks one's own faults and points out the glaring flaws of someone else. For example, listen to the conversations you have with your mate. If you hear some common themes that stand out such as a nagging or whining tone, ask God to help you correct it. If you find yourself with a prickly tongue that constantly spews out sarcasm or disgust, just remember that it is hard to stick to a porcupine.

Finally, the phrase "one flesh" refers to sexual union between a husband and wife. God has declared that you and your husband are to be that way—one flesh. Because the word "flesh" refers to the physical body, this verse is referring to the sexual union of a man and a wife. Isn't that interesting? When a man leaves his father and mother and unites with his wife in marriage, the very first thing they are instructed to do is to enjoy the physical union that allows them to be one flesh.

Most newlyweds don't have to be told this, but the more mature crowd may need a little reminder! For older couples, Proverbs 5:18 speaks to the husband: *"Let your fountain be blessed, and rejoice in the wife of your youth."* What is he going to do if his wife doesn't want to be blessed by his fountain? He has a commandment to obey in which she also has a part. The fact that this verse refers to a man who is married to the wife of his youth means that they are no longer young; they have grown older together. The verse points to the longevity of a relationship. The intention here is to help older people understand that their age is no reason why they should not continue to enjoy each other sexually. Enjoy your responsibility, ladies!

When God joined Adam and Eve in holy matrimony, their sexual access was unlimited. In the book of Genesis, we read, *"And the man and his wife were both naked and were not ashamed"* (Genesis 2:25). Adam and Eve were constantly together and always available for the enjoyment of each other. There were no rules and no inhibitions. He enjoyed her body, and she enjoyed his. They never felt any shame because there was nothing to be ashamed of. They did not think any less of each other or despise each other because they were naked.

The body carries great importance because God created it. The first thing sin affected was the man and the woman's need to cover their physical bodies. The curse of sin immediately affected their relationship with each other, which caused them to hide their nakedness. Why else did they run to make covering for themselves after they sinned in Genesis 3:7? When their eyes were open to good and evil, wicked thoughts immediately entered their minds—they immediately knew that they had done wrong. Because their bodies were not covered up, they no longer held each other with the high esteem to which they were accustomed.

Particularly after you've been together for a while, be careful to continue holding him up with high regard. When he disrobes, don't send him the message that you are not satisfied with what you see. For that matter, you may be feeling self-conscious with your own body, thinking that it's not good enough to be enjoyed by your husband.

Maybe you know he doesn't like the few extra pounds, and so you want to get your body straight before you offer it to him. Don't be deceived. Don't hide from him and do not let him hide from you. It would be better to bring these issues out in the open where the two of you can work through them. If you bring it before the Lord, He will show you the solution.

You may have noticed that the first thing that can go out the window when you and your husband have a disagreement is physical intimacy. Ephesians 4:26–27 says, *"Be angry, and yet do not sin; do not let the sun go down on your anger, and do not give the devil an opportunity."* This Scripture is clear that we are to not let our anger linger indefinitely. When you obey this commandment, it keeps you from damaging a major aspect of your relationship.

There is risk involved when two mates are distanced because of their disagreements. It leaves space for the enemy to get in between the two partners and feed them evil thoughts. Be very careful; the devil is extremely crafty, and he only desires to destroy your relationship.

The Bible issues a wise warning: don't give him an opportunity to wreak havoc in your marriage.

Your issue might be that you don't feel like enjoying your husband in a physical way. You are tired at the end of the day, and you just don't want to be bothered. I have news for you: you don't have to feel like it. Romance is nice, but it is not necessary. Feeling "turned on" (if I may be so base) is nice, but it is not necessary either. Obedience is what is necessary. Why? The sexual act is not just about you. It is about obeying and honoring God in your marriage.

God is concerned about the quality of your union. Listen to the warning He gives, as it identifies God's concern: "*Stop depriving one another, except by agreement for a time, so that you may devote yourselves to prayer, and come together again so that Satan will not tempt you because of your lack of self-control*" (1 Corinthians 7:5–6). Satan is your enemy, and he wants to destroy you, your children, and your legacy. If you and your husband are not engaging in sexual activity on a regular basis, you are leaving yourselves open for a disaster.

Even if you have to, say to yourself, "I'm going to make a choice to do this in obedience, even though I don't feel like it." Then just do it. It won't be the first thing you did that you didn't feel like doing. The Word of God explains it this way, "*The husband must fulfill his duty to his wife, and likewise also the wife to her husband. The wife does not have authority over her own body, but the husband does; and likewise also the husband does not have authority over his own body, but the wife does*" (1 Corinthians 7:3–4).

When you took your wedding vows, you essentially gave up your personal rights to your body and became obligated to your husband. The reverse is also true; he is obligated to you in every way. Furthermore, when you are obedient to God's design for your union you benefit from what you give in the sexual union. Could it be that some of the problems you are having in your marriage right now are related to the lack of activity in your bedroom? Hmmm . . . think about that.

There should be a mutual give-and-take as it was in the beginning when God created the first couple. The essence of the sexual union is intended to be the deepest expression of selfless love and consideration between a man and his wife. Even when you don't "feel like it," you are commanded to regularly exercise care and concern for each other through your physical unity. God will reward your willing obedience to Him. When you submit to the Lord, He will honor you.

You might say, "I disagree. I shouldn't do what I don't want to do." You may certainly disagree. But God's Word rules; it is the law of nature. Your disagreement does not change God's authority to rule. God's Word is true. If you obey it, you will be blessed by it. If you disobey it, sooner or later you will reap the repercussions of your actions.

AS FAR AS IT GOES: LIMITATIONS ON MARRIAGE

Marriage is a permanent state for this life, but it doesn't exist in the next one. The purpose of marriage is to be a reflection of the relationship between Christ and His Church. As such, it is designed for God's glory. But marriage does have limitations.

What limitations does it have? It is limited by what can be done in alignment with God's Word. If your husband asks you to do something that contradicts the Word of God, don't do it. Marriage is limited by what God says. Does your husband want to have a wife-swapping party? Your answer is no—that is not in line with the Word of God. Does he think that watching porn with you will spice up your sex life? You may legitimately decline—it does not line up with the Word of God.

Is he physically abusing you or sexually abusing your children? You need to take immediate action to protect yourself and your family. You are not required to compromise God's laws and expose yourself or your child to evil. You may answer his behavior with a resounding no if he has crossed a boundary identified in the Word of God. And do not worry; God will take care of you.

Ultimately, the Lord God is your provider, your encourager, and your protector. You have one God and one husband. Furthermore, they are not one and the same. Your husband is not God. Don't confuse God's role with the role that your husband is to assume in your marriage. Know the Word of God and the things that He provides through His Word and do not look to your husband to meet all your needs. He is not the source of all your blessings. In teaching the believers, the apostle Paul said of the Lord, *"My God will supply all your needs according to His riches in glory in Christ Jesus"* (Philippians 4:19). Look to God to provide for you the things that God did not equip your husband to give you.

Nevertheless, the more that your husband aligns himself with God, the more the Lord can bless you through him. But when you mistakenly put your husband in God's place, you have made him an idol. God is your God. Your husband is your friend, your partner, your coworker, the one to whom you submit, the one you honor, and the one you serve. As he follows God, you follow him.

LIVING BY THE COVENANT

Every solid organization must have a sound structure. The issue is not who is in charge, but who has overall responsibility. That is why it is critical to follow what God says about the order of the home. Just as in a company structure, each member has a responsibility. In the family organizational structure, the authority over the household is a function of the responsibility that God has given the husband. Paul addresses this issue and sets the proper order in Ephesians 5:23, *"For the husband is the head of the wife, as Christ also is the head of the church, He Himself being the Savior of the body."* In other words, God appointed the husband as the chief executive officer (CEO). He is to be the head.

What this means for an unmarried woman who is planning to marry someday is to make sure you choose a man that you can follow. Just like a bad CEO can sink a company, a husband who is not fulfilling his duties can devastate his family. A CEO who won't apply himself can bankrupt a company, and a husband who won't work can ruin his family's finances. A grouchy and mean CEO will produce a negative corporate culture in the same way that a disagreeable husband can create a negative environment in his home.

Moreover, a CEO who dresses well and is charming—but offers nothing significant to back him up—will lead his company into disaster. In a similar way, a husband who selfishly puts his needs before his wife and children's needs will sorely neglect his family.

In order for a family to function properly the man must assume the proper role as the head of the family. If he doesn't exert his God-given authority, there will be chaos. Without a final authority in the home, a husband and wife are probably not getting along. For every decision on which they disagree, there will be two people negotiating who will get their way. That creates chaos.

In His wisdom, God implemented this hierarchal structure after the fall of man in Genesis. Before that, it was not necessary because there was no sin. Now that sin has entered the picture, everyone wants his way. In Genesis, chapter 3, God set the hierarchical structure to reestablish order. In His discipline of the woman, He placed her husband over her. That is the context for the command He issued in Colossians 3:18, *"Wives, be subject to your husbands, as is fitting in the Lord."*

It is important to note that the second part of Ephesians 1:23 says that Christ is the Savior of the body. Christ is the only one who can save you. Your husband can encourage you spiritually, but he can't save you. That's not his job. It is the Holy Spirit who will help you mature in God, grow you in Him, and bring you to the spiritual point to which you need to arrive. Don't expect, or allow, your husband to be an intermediary between you and God. If you do, when he fails, you will fail too.

On the other hand, your husband is responsible for your physical care. He is to provide for your physical needs. It is his job to take care of you. You should look good because of him. Your health should be taken care of because of him. Your hair and your appearance should always be intact because of him. You should have food in the refrigerator because of him.

But some women will say, "Well, I work and provide those things for myself. I don't need any authority over me." Maybe you do take care of yourself. That's wonderful. I was raised to be independent too. But the fact is, biblically, you and I are not responsible for our physical needs, our husbands are. So, if you and your husband decide that you should not, or cannot do those things for yourself—your husband is responsible for doing them.

God doesn't assign titles without also giving responsibility. The fact that the man is the head of the home is not meant to insult you; it is meant to make sure that you have what you need in order to maximize your life. The structure is placed there for your benefit. It is God's way of aligning you and your husband with the order of creation.

In some cases, a husband is disabled and can't work and, therefore, cannot fulfill his function properly. Then, certainly, the wife will need to take care of him and assume responsibility of the family's needs. But his disability doesn't necessarily let him off the hook, so you shouldn't let him off the hook either. That doesn't mean nag him; rather, you should respect him, encourage him, and expect him to maximize his abilities in accordance with his capabilities and condition in life. Listen to what God says about your relationship, *"Nevertheless each individual among you also is to love his own wife even as himself, and the wife must see to it that she respects her husband"* (Ephesians 5:33). Don't become discouraged and give up on him.

And, speaking of not giving up, find some girlfriends to support you! You might need their encouragement to build your own strength. Let him know that he has some responsibilities in the relationship, and give him the space to fulfill them in the ways that he can do so. Don't dishonor him just because he may be in a disadvantaged position. He's still the head of the home, and he is still responsible for you and your children. Encourage him to find ways that he can be productive. No matter what circumstances surround the two of you, the message is: don't give up on each other.

YOUR ATTITUDE

Are you so defensive and sensitive that you are just waiting for him to say something so that you can jump down his throat? Do you have a disposition that says, "Don't step on my toes, or you'll wish that you hadn't"? Well, God's Word has an answer for you, *"A constant dripping on a day of steady rain and a contentious woman are alike"* (Proverbs 27:15).

One day, I was watching a television show where they were applauding women who have an angry and contentious attitude. These women were being called by a name that I would dare not repeat. The premise was that women who embrace this position can get things done. However, the participants on the program overlooked the fact that women with such abusive characteristics are often experiencing life trauma.

As a result, they have been unable to maintain solid marriages, raise rebellious children, and live their lives within a tormented environment. What good is getting things done if you have all that negativity going on? There are viable alternatives through which you can still get things done. An old adage wisely says, "You can catch more flies with honey than with vinegar."

Pride is often the source of contention. Listen to how Scripture describes a person who is prideful, *"In the mouth of the foolish is a rod of pride: but the lips of the wise shall preserve them"* (Proverbs 14:3 KJV). Sometimes it is obvious when a person opens her mouth and says whatever happens to be on her mind. People who are unwise do not give consideration to what they say and feel as though they are justified in saying whatever they want. They do so without thinking first. Most of the time, their words are cutting and insensitive. They are putting their words before someone else's feelings—and that is a matter of pride.

When prideful words proceed from the mouth, they act like a rod and beat up anyone who is in their path. Not only do such words batter coworkers, they abuse children, husbands, and friends alike. Then when one prideful mouth encounters another, a bloody battle ensues. You may have witnessed such battles in a meeting, in board-rooms, and around water fountains. Sometimes these battles are even waged in the church. They tear down and do not build up anyone involved. The result of such battles is the destruction of both parties.

Rather, you should train your mind and mouth so that, before you speak, you determine how to communicate in a way that matches your intended meaning. The lips are the last point of contact that your words have with the world. Keep them closed until you have thoroughly evaluated what you plan to say. If you always have to get the last word and will argue to the end, you have a problem that must be worked out with the Lord's help. He will teach you how to give up your mouth of pride and exchange it for one that pleases Him. You will learn there is a better way to communicate by following this advice, *"A gentle answer turns away wrath, but a harsh word stirs up anger"* (Proverbs 15:1).

DEAR PRUDENCE

A prudent woman is one who has a good head on her shoulders. She demonstrates balance in her judgment and uses her insight to determine how things can best be accomplished. As a result, her family prospers because of her creativity and intuition. Proverbs 19:14 says, *"House and wealth are an inheritance from fathers, but a prudent wife is from the Lord."* You can determine if the Lord is satisfied with your ways by considering these questions. Do you make good choices with money, or do you spend every dime you get as quickly as you can? Do you make decisions that will benefit the family, even if you have to make short-term sacrifices?

When my husband and I first got married, we quickly got into debt. When we made the decision to pay it off and live debt-free, I presented my husband with a plan on how we could do it. Eventually, we got out of debt—but not by using the method that I had proposed. However, it was a blessing that we managed to get out of debt when we did, because being debt-free allowed me to stay at home with my children for an extended period of time.

Twenty-six years later, we were out to dinner one evening. My husband said to the couple with whom we were dining, "Karia has always had good ideas. When we first got married, I didn't always listen to her. But over the years, I've come to realize she has a pretty good business head. Now I really value her input." Then he referenced the incident about our finances which happened over two decades earlier!

Ladies, sometimes it takes awhile for your insight to be accepted! The ability to act in prudent ways is a blessing from God. Keep working diligently to promote the best interest of your family. Don't become discouraged. Your labor of love will eventually produce fruit.

DIVORCE: THE UGLY SIDE OF MARRIAGE

There is more at stake than you think. If you are experiencing serious trouble in your marriage, listen to what the Word of the Lord has to say to those who contemplate the idea of divorce.

> *This is another thing you do: you cover the altar of the Lord with tears, with weeping and with groaning, because He no longer regards the offering or accepts it with favor from your hand.*
>
> *Yet you say, "For what reason?" Because the Lord has been a witness between you and the wife of your youth, against whom you have dealt treacherously, though she is your companion and your wife by covenant.*
>
> *But not one has done so who has a remnant of the Spirit and what did that one do while he was seeking a godly offspring? Take heed then to your spirit, and let no one deal treacherously against the wife of your youth.*
>
> *"For I hate divorce," says the Lord, the God of Israel, "and him who covers his garment with wrong," says the Lord of hosts. So take heed to your spirit, that you do not deal treacherously.* (Malachi 2:13–16)

In biblical times, the children of Israel had a problem. They thought that they were doing all the right stuff, but they were not experiencing God's blessing in their lives. They couldn't understand why God wasn't blessing them. Then God spoke through His prophet and told them why they were not doing well. He told them that their behavior was not pleasant in His sight. They offered God sacrifices, but He did not accept them because their hearts were not right and their motives were wrong.

They were expecting something in return from God, but the Lord God had a problem with the way the people were taking their marriages so lightly. God takes marriage very seriously and His people were not acting accordingly. Marriage is a covenant shared by three partners: a husband, a wife, and God Himself. It is an institution that He created, and He personally witnesses every marriage. The husband and wife are to consider their marriage a contract that they made with God. They are to honor Him by performing their respective duties according to the terms of their contract.

I have presented many of the details of God's marriage laws already in this chapter. But please read them in detail. They can be found in the book of Ephesians, chapter 5, and 1 Corinthians, chapter 7. Study and meditate on them often so that you will not be found guilty in a similar way to the people of ancient times. You want the sacrifices that you offer God to be acceptable to Him.

God's Spirit inhabits even the smallest details of marriage. And when people mistakenly abuse their spouses and their vows, He is not happy. He adamantly proclaims, "I hate divorce!" He cautions those who are married not to "deal treacherously" with their spouses. God was speaking to men who would act like traitors to their wives by mistreating them and turning their backs on the Lord. That phrase includes everything that could bring harm to a woman, but most of all, divorce and abandonment. So watch yourselves. Don't let your guard down and possibly destroy your marriage. Don't cheat.

God hates divorce. It has a negative effect on His succession plan. He wants to build His kingdom generation by generation through your children. Give Him a chance to do that.

However, I must point out that God does allow divorce in two cases: adultery or abandonment. On the subject of adultery, Jesus stated the following, *"It was said, 'whoever sends his wife away, let him give her a certificate of divorce'; but I say to you that everyone who divorces his wife, except for the reason of unchastity, makes her commit adultery; and whoever marries a divorced woman commits adultery"* (Matthew 5:31–32).

God will accept divorce for the reason of marital infidelity perpetrated by the man or the woman. Second, the only other reason God will allow divorce is for abandonment. Scripture explains, *"If the unbelieving one leaves, let him leave; the brother or the sister is not under bondage in such cases, but God has called us to peace"* (1 Corinthians 7:15). In the case of a marriage between a believer and one who does not profess Christ, God will allow the believing spouse to be in agreement with a divorce when the unbeliever no longer wants to be in the relationship. That is considered abandonment.

Many times a marriage between a believer and a nonbeliever is not on one accord. Discord and strife can easily enter into the picture. They cannot agree because they have opposite perspectives on life. There is no peace in a household where two unhappy people are constantly fighting against each other. God acknowledges this and releases the believing person from trying to stay in the relationship if the other spouse wants to call it quits. Otherwise, there will be no peace; and as God's Word puts it, *"God has called us to peace."*

There is one final note on this serious subject. Abuse of any kind is unacceptable. I believe that God would also consider such heinous behavior as "dealing treacherously" with his wife. If your husband is guilty of this, talk to a qualified counselor or some other trustworthy person. If you are being abused, seek help by all means. This would constitute abandonment by your husband of his biblical responsibility to take good care of you and your family. Because of his mistreatment, you may have a biblical reason for divorce.

As far as God is concerned, if your reason for divorce isn't either of these two reasons, you are not divorced in His sight. You can get all the paper you want, but He says you are still married. Marriage is the first institution that God created. He doesn't intend for you to destroy it for your own convenience. If you try, the destruction that may come as a result may, in some ways, destroy you.

FUNCTIONS—HIS AND HERS

God gave Adam the job of taking care of the Garden. Adam cultivated the ground and watched over the vegetation that it produced. As such, Adam was given the responsibility to be the provider of the family. God then created Eve to function as Adam's partner—his helper. However, her role is not secondary in any way. She was created to complement him and be Adam's companion.

After Adam and Eve were found guilty of disobeying God, He showed His displeasure to them both. Since God had already blessed Adam and Eve (Genesis 1:28), He would not curse them. But He did issue them severe punishments that were appropriate for their respective roles. Adam's function was in the field; he would now have to sweat and labor with the ground to maximize his productivity.

Taking into consideration the fact that Eve's ability to bear children would be the way in which she and Adam would be fruitful and multiply, the area in which Eve was called to maximize her productivity was in the home. Her very name, Eve, was designed with family in mind. It means "the mother of all living." Although bringing children into the world is a joyous occasion, God told Eve that her happiness would be marred by pain and sorrow when she brought forth children. Eve came to understand what God meant as she began to produce her children. However, God is infinite in His mercy. To redeem her from the disastrous decision she had made, God promised Eve that through her seed would come the Messiah: Jesus, our Lord and Savior.

Many centuries later, women continue to reflect the female characteristics of our foremother, Eve. In fact, our priorities bear resemblance to those of the first woman of creation. Particularly for those who are married and have produced a family, we have a certain function to carry out within the household. The distinctions between the functions of the husband and wife may have blurred over time as the economy dictates that two incomes are far more useful than one. As a result, many women have taken on additional responsibilities; yet, God's institution and framework of a marriage remains unchanged.

Just as He wanted the women of antiquity to follow His pattern, God still desires women today to maintain our overall function. Therefore, through His wisdom and forethought, He provided instructions to assist women in carrying out our priorities: *"Older women likewise are to be reverent in their behavior, not malicious gossips nor enslaved to much wine, teaching what is good, so that they may encourage the young women to love their husbands, to love their children, to be sensible, pure, workers at home, kind, being subject to their own husbands, so that the word of God will not be dishonored"* (Titus 2:3–5).

The Word of God is very clear that the woman's primary responsibility is caring for her family. You should understand that your family comes first. The way that you keep this objective intact is by being determined that you will always consider your family before any other person or circumstance. Then implement that decision day by day.

Sometimes it will be hard to put your family first, because it will cost you something. But make every effort to keep doing it and it will pay off later. Not only will you bring honor to God by your actions, it is a strong way of showing love to your husband and your children. They will observe when you make sacrifices on their behalf. They will grow to appreciate you and the choices that you make with them in mind.

The problem with some women is that they emotionally or physically abandon their home in exchange for their career work. These women have a choice whether they want to work or not; yet, they choose to work over staying at home. Sure, going to work may be much more rewarding for you than changing diapers, washing dishes, sorting laundry, or paying bills. Someone at work might actually say "thank you" when you do a good job. But that does not give you the right to change your primary investment from your home to your workplace. Your family comes first.

Biblically, it is the husband's responsibility to care for the home financially. But some women must carry the stress of providing financially for their family. They would prefer to be at home full-time for their children; but unfortunately, they can't afford to do so. I say to these women, although you may be in a challenging situation, be encouraged, God has equipped you to fulfill your responsibilities— and He will see you through.

If you're being forced to figure everything out yourself, that is stressful. If your husband needs a job so that he can provide for his family, pray that God will strengthen your husband and show him the way to find one. God will present the truth of His Word to him so that his eyes will be opened. There is nothing too hard for God; He can lead your husband to find employment. Trust the Lord and continue to respect your husband. When God blesses him to take care of his family financially, give the responsibility back to him as soon as you can.

It is true that women are not only versatile; we are great multi-taskers. In addition to our primary duty as mother and nurturer of the home, God has well-equipped us to be successful in many other ways. Throughout biblical history, the woman had a number of responsibilities in the Old Testament. Yet, her primary responsibility was always that of taking care of her household. As early as the book of Genesis, women handled domestic concerns and prepared meals (see Genesis 18:6).

With skillful hands, she produced fine clothing (Exodus 35:25–26; Proverbs 31:24; Acts 9:39). She lovingly cared for children (Exodus 2:9–10; Proverbs 31:28; Titus 2:4). As a businesswoman and real estate investor, she produced income (Acts 16:14; Proverbs 31:16–18) and worked in fields for food (Ruth 2:2–3). She functioned in ministry (2 Kings 22:14; 2 Chronicles 34:22; Matthew 27:56, 61; Mark 15:40; Acts 18:18, 26; 1 Corinthians 16:19). She led an army and ruled in government (Judges 4:4–5).

Through all of these examples, women have demonstrated their capability of exercising dominion over the earth. You are probably doing many of these functions already in your role as wife and mother, but consider whether it is time to join with your husband to exercise dominion over the earth in other ways that God has called you. That means that the two of you need to spend time in prayer, seeking God's will and wisdom. Then take God's direction into serious consideration, set your goals together, and give your all to achieving them. You do not have to be afraid if the choices you make are based on your faith that God has called you and equipped you to accomplish His purposes.

But, as a final word of caution, keep in mind that all of God's purposes do not have to be accomplished in one day. This is why it's crucial to be sensitive to God's timing. There will be different stages in your life, with different levels of freedom and availability. The period right after childbirth may not be the best time to start a career with travel demands. You won't be able to spend the proper amount of time with your baby and see to his or her development. Instead, this would be a time when God wants you to provide your child with physical and spiritual nurturing. And for that, you must be present in the critical bonding process with your new baby.

In other words, your decisions in life may not always be based merely on your ability to do a particular thing; instead, timing, priorities, and God's immediate expectation for your life is most important. God's purpose for you at any time of your life is made clear in His Word. It is part of His overall design for your life. As you develop and strengthen your intimate relationship with your Daddy—He will lead you and guide you into the path of victory that has already been laid out for you.

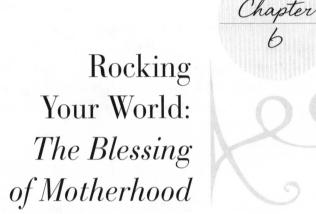

Rocking Your World: *The Blessing of Motherhood*

*I*n the late 1700s, a group of mothers across this land decided to raise powerful children that could impact the world. Their children would be model citizens and know how to sacrifice for the benefit of others. At that time, only boys received an education. However, this group of women decided they would educate their girls too. As the idea caught on and spread throughout the nation, they raised their children to diligently study Scripture, read insightful books, analyze newspaper articles, and review scholarly publications to encourage them and develop their critical thinking skills.

America was a new country at the time; it was called the Republic of America. The title eventually given to the parenting style of these goal-oriented mothers was "republican motherhood." Their children grew up to be amazing men and women. In fact, they helped to establish the democratic principles on which this country was built.

God is looking for a group of mothers who will raise children to influence the world for His kingdom in this era. These kingdom-building mothers will educate their children well, teaching them how to discern truth from error. Members of this special motherhood will nurture their children and guide them in pursuing God's purposes. Always putting their children first, kingdom-building mothers will delay accomplishing their own personal goals when they conflict with the responsibilities of raising godly children.

The kingdom mother may not climb the career ladder according to the status quo. That is not her focus. But this mother will later find the children whom she rocked in her arms will soon rock the world with the message of the gospel.

WHO IS THE ADULT?

As the adult, you have been given the responsibility to raise your child. However, he or she may not want to cooperate with your plans and ideas. He may be an independent-minded individual with his own agenda. She may be demanding and selfishly want to do things her way. Both of these situations set up a conflict, which ultimately you have to win. That's what it means to raise a child—you set the rules and guide them; it cannot be the other way around.

Childrearing can be quite a challenge. In the thick of a confrontation, how often do we look at them and think, *Gee, you are a magnificent creation. You are such a blessing!* Usually, our focus is on asking why they threw that graham cracker on the floor, why they think we're unaware that they intentionally forgot to put their boots on, or who they think is paying for the room that they consider their sole possession.

Sisters, in the midst of all this, God says that your children are a blessing. Listen to the profound words that He pronounced over the creation of His human species: *". . . and God said to them, 'Be fruitful and multiply, and fill the earth, and subdue it . . . '"* (Genesis 1:28). However, there are even more blessings to be attained in this wonderful story of life. The Word of God describes the fruit that we produce in this way. *"Lo, children are an heritage of the Lord; and the fruit of the womb is his reward"* (Psalm 127:3 KJV).

The word "heritage" in this verse is referring to an inheritance—something given to an individual that holds great value and promise. Your children are an inheritance from your heavenly Father. They are a gift that He has passed down from Himself to you. They are His gift, and God expects you to invest in your children from the very moment that you receive them.

If you continue until they mature and leave the comfortable nest which you provide, they will eventually comfort you when you are lonely. As you and your children grow older, they will encourage you when you are down and make sure that your needs are met. Scripture assures us in this way, *"Train up a child in the way he should go, even when he is old he will not depart from it"* (Proverbs 22:6). From the moment a child is born, this should be our motivation.

The Bible says that the fruit of the womb is a reward. The word "reward" also means wages. What are the wages for? What did you do to earn your children? You were obedient to God's command to be fruitful and multiply. Obedience to God produces blessings.

In spite of the graham cracker issues, the stubborn response "No!" at the age of two, the all-night emergency room visits, the endless stream of outgoing allowances, the teenage tussles over dating, the insistence that they load and unload the dishwasher, the tutoring, pleading, and homework reminders—despite all of this—you know in your heart that your children are a blessing.

PROTECTING YOUR INTERESTS

Your children are also your powerful weapon. Scripture says, *"As arrows are in the hand of a mighty man; so are children of the youth"* (Psalm 127:4 KJV). The bow and arrow was a weapon to be feared in the ancient world. The arrow was lethal because of its element of surprise. It could be launched from a hidden place, as in an ambush, or shot from different angles. Its versatility made it a potent weapon against any enemy.

Your children will be your defense later on in life. Have you ever noticed something like the following scenario? Or perhaps you have had this experience with an elderly parent: a loved one is lying in a hospital room. An adult child shows up and begins to ask questions of the nurse, "What kind of medicine is she on?" "I need to speak with the doctor." "I'm curious about why . . . " These are the words of a concerned child. You could say that they represent an arrow being shot on behalf of a parent in need. Suddenly, that person has created an environment of accountability and expects to hear the proper responses. As a result, the ailing parent can rest more peacefully—their inheritance is now taking care of them.

Recently, we were negotiating to buy a beautiful piece of property. I wasn't sure if the Lord would give it to us, but we fell in love with it. It is not far from a main highway, but the area has a country-like atmosphere. There are several houses on the land, and a gravel road travels from the front of the property to the back. At the rear, there is a stable that can house several horses with enough pasture for grazing.

The owner of the property is an older gentleman. He and his wife are as nice as they can be. Having built his financial empire over the course of many years in real estate development, they have amassed a great deal of wealth. At this point in his life, he has wisely placed his property in a family trust. Although I could tell that he liked us, he made it clear from the beginning of our negotiations that he would not be the final decision maker.

He told us, "I have nine children and they are the officers of the trust. One of my children is a lawyer. Another is a real estate agent. Another one is a Certified Public Accountant, and one is a builder. They don't let me make decisions. They tell me, 'Daddy, we'll handle this.'"

He jokingly admits, "They don't even let me pick my own socks." This man loves his family. He spent years investing in them. And now that he is older and retired, they are able to care for him. Moreover, they protect his assets. They use their fields of expertise to reject anything that would not be in their father's best interest. God blessed him with enough children to protect him in different ways. They will manage his estate with excellence because they are his inheritance.

That's what the wisdom of God means as it declares, *"Happy is the man that hath his quiver full of them: they shall not be ashamed, but they shall speak with the enemies in the gate"* (Psalm 127:5 KJV). The *New American Standard Bible* version uses the word "warrior" in this text instead of the word "man." A warrior fights to accomplish something, to win a battle. As a result, you can interpret this verse in this way: "Happy is the warrior whose home, or quiver, is full of children."

One might ask, why would someone want to have a house full of children? There is no shame in having many children, as long as the parents are walking in obedience to God's Word. According to God's intended way, children grow up and live out the investment you made in them. They will be loyal to their parents and contribute their skills and abilities to the cause of the family. There are many examples where a family business is passed down from one generation to another. The older parents train each new age group, and the succession continues. Both parents and children alike benefit from the inheritance handed down from the previous generation.

A gate in biblical times was the "public square" of modern times. Being one of the most frequented places in town, it was where legal, civil, and community activities took place. Today more than ever, people prey on the elderly and they need protection. God intends for a man's offspring to serve as his gate of defense, successfully warding off anyone who may think about taking advantage of him. It should be an established family agreement that intruders and legitimate people alike have to conduct their business with an older person's children and speak with them about any of their concerns.

My mother-in-law was a single parent with seven children. Now they are all adults, and she doesn't have to worry about a thing. Although she does so simply because she is a worrier, there is no need for her to concern herself. Every day, one of her children comes over to her house to check on her. She also has many grandchildren and great-grandchildren that adore her. If she becomes ill, somebody is always there for her. If anyone bothers her about anything, there will be four or five people immediately coming to her rescue.

My husband has flown in to take her to a doctor's appointment that she didn't want to keep. Our children adore "Granny." She loves with all her heart and shares hugs and kisses, roast beef, and pumpkin pie. When her children were very young, I'm sure it wasn't a fun thing to raise seven children alone. But, as tough as life was in rural Virginia for a single mom, today her investment is paying off.

What does a "full" quiver look like for you? Maybe it isn't seven children . . . but, then again, maybe it is. This is a decision to be made by a wife and her husband. However, through His Word, God wants everyone to be aware of the long-term benefits of having a home filled with children and the happiness such an environment can bring.

Moreover, Scripture teaches the opposite of what today's culture espouses. Society will try to tell you that children can prevent you from winning your battles or pursuing your dreams. Through the heavy influence of media, the image portrayed is that children take up too much time and energy. There is a false perception that says the fewer children you have, the happier and more productive you will be.

The Bible says that children will keep you from being ashamed as you battle to accomplish your goals in life. Your children are to be your ally, not your enemy. Just remember that the commandment to have children is a potential blessing for those who obey, not a bother. These days, much is spoken about the importance of fulfilling our destiny in God. It is true; God does have a plan for your life, and He intends to accomplish it. But as you "subdue the earth," understand that you are to subdue it for generations to come, not just for your generation.

In other words, if God gives you the ability to have children and invest in them—they will bring a reward. Yes, raising children can be a difficult process. As you contemplate the possibility, there are many concerns to consider. What if they turn out badly?

Adam and Eve were learning to adapt to their new circumstances when their first two boys were born. Those boys made life hard. One of them turned out to be a murderer, and the other was good, but too trusting. The good one was killed by the bad one. God sent him into solitary confinement away from the family. Yet, Adam and Eve continued to be obedient. They had another son, Seth. Eventually, their children populated the earth. It is because of their obedience to "be fruitful and multiply" that we exist.

Many years ago, the first couple set an example for us, and we are to follow the same command. For example, my grandmother and grandfather, Andrew Beatrice Williams and Malvin Isaiah Williams, had two children: my mother and my uncle. In turn, my mother had two children and my uncle had five. My mother's children produced four, and my cousins produced thirteen. From two original children, there are seven grandchildren and nineteen great-grandchildren. That is the kind of multiplication that God desires. It is the way that He intends for His gospel message to spread across the earth.

My uncle intentionally sought to multiply his family. He would walk through his house on holidays, laughing and commanding, "Be fruitful and multiply!" By doing this, he encouraged his children to have children.

Are you preparing your children to multiply, according to God's Word? If you are a single mother, wondering how all of this applies to you, I say, be a mother with purpose. While you are working, place your children in the care of those who will look after them and teach them about Christ. And when you are not working, be at home with the children. Take them shopping with you and teach them how to spend wisely. Invest time to ensure that your children are successful in school. Set a reading quota and assign books that they must read by a certain time.

Sometimes it may seem easier to be passive and let your children have their way. It takes energy to discipline them and not let up until they have correctly learned the principle that you're trying to get across. It's time consuming to sit with them and talk about your goals and expectations for them. Yet, these things are all too important not to invest yourself and accomplish them.

Speaking of discipline, young boys need good role models to follow.

If you don't already know someone who can set the right example for your children, pray and ask the Lord to provide someone. It is God's will that children are taught and brought up properly. He will answer that prayer for you and show you the right person that you can entrust with this responsibility. By all means, please do not give up on disciplining your children. The stakes are too high and their future is too important. Your labor of love will soon pay off.

In God's eyes, you must realize how important you are. You are the vehicle through which God will promote His kingdom, and the impact of your efforts will continue to increase over time. You will witness the fruit of your effort. Your child could be the next Barack Obama, Billy Graham, or Ben Carson. Let's practice kingdom-building motherhood. God will be pleased as we seek to achieve the result He is looking for: filling the earth and subduing it.

DADDY'S GIRL AND MOMMY'S BOY

For parents, playing favorites can be a dangerous game. There is a story in the Bible about twin brothers: Jacob and Esau. Even before they were born, the two boys didn't get along. They were fighting in the womb, and their mother, Rebekah, thought something was terribly wrong. So she prayed and asked the Lord about it. The Lord said that there were two nations in her womb, and both of them were fighting for first place. He also declared that the younger one would prevail. During Rebekah's labor and the babies' delivery, they were still fighting. Ouch!

After they were born, Mommy Rebekah and Daddy Isaac didn't help to improve the situation very much. The parents did something that often causes trouble in families: they chose favorites between their two children. Scripture recorded the account, *"When the boys grew up, Esau became a skillful hunter, a man of the field, but Jacob was a peaceful man, living in tents. Now Isaac loved Esau, because he had a taste for game, but Rebekah loved Jacob"* (Genesis 25:27–28).

As the boys grew up, they began to adopt traits and habits that reminded the parents of themselves. Isaac noticed that he favored Esau, the older of the two, because of the boy's rough, hairy exterior. He was an aggressive type who liked to hunt. However, Isaac did not appreciate the way that Jacob was developing. In Old Testament culture, it was the woman's job to maintain the home, cook the dinner, and remain inside the tents. His father probably wondered, *Why is Jacob always in the tent?*

Rebekah noticed the same thing about her son. She saw that he had taken an interest in preparing meals and enjoyed working alongside her in their home. She was pleased with Jacob and encouraged his domestic abilities. Rebekah also saw her husband's favoritism, and her maternal instincts naturally took up for her gentle-mannered son.

Jacob was her boy. It was nice having company in the kitchen. After all, she didn't have a daughter, her husband worked all the time, and her other son was always running around in the field somewhere. This one loved her. When she needed assistance, he saw it and helped her. He gave her a hug when she was lonely. He saw her tears when nobody was around.

If she discovered something new, in excitement she would call, "Jacob!" He would run to her and share in her enthusiasm. They would laugh together. If she burned her hand while cooking, she would scream and he would be the one to hear it. He was the one to lovingly nurse her back to health.

When it came time for her husband to pronounce his blessing over their elder son, Rebekah immediately took action. Rightfully, the blessing belonged to Esau and if there had been no objection and subsequent intervention, Esau would have claimed his inheritance. But their mother wasn't about to allow Esau to get an advantage over her favored one. She helped Jacob just as he had helped her so many times.

Although legally she had no voice in this time-honored tradition, she cleverly devised a way to award the family inheritance to her favorite son, Jacob. The plot that she executed with her son was successful; together they had managed to steal Esau's birthright inheritance.

If you have a favorite in your family, it is probably the one who draws closest to you. Maybe you have a son who enjoys grocery shopping with you and going to the bank. He just seems to like being around you. But your favoritism feels like rejection to another child, and a conflict may be brewing. Siblings need to feel equally loved by their parents. Favoritism hurts and the pain lasts a lifetime.

Jacob and Esau's descendants fought for generations. Eventually, Esau became the father of the Edomites. When David was king, he fought the Edomites to establish the kingdom for the Israelites, the descendants of Jacob.

If you don't want a divided family reunion, do not foster feelings in any of your children that lead them to feel less loved by you. For example, sometimes marital problems produce favorites. Because Daddy doesn't get enough attention from you, he gets it from his daughter. When your daughter senses a disproportionate amount of affection, she behaves as though she can do no wrong. If another child is observing the situation, this is a catastrophe waiting to happen. All children need the balanced love and discipline of both parents.

Frequently, parents make the mistake of looking at their children simply as "little people," who do not posses the understanding to recognize when they are being wronged. On the contrary, it is not as though their feelings have not developed to the point of absorbing the impact of negative treatment. My grandfather used to say, "Little acorns grow up to be oak trees." Children have the same heart, muscles, arteries, bones, and brain capacity that they will have as adults. Indeed, they are little people, but they are fully people at the same time. It is not as though you can wait until they are adults before you deal with their full array of human instincts and emotions.

During a recent visit to a nursing home, I observed an interaction that was intriguing to me. There was a fairly large man who could physically not sit straight. He leaned over the side of his wheelchair at almost a 45-degree angle. As he was wheeling himself around, he passed by me. He also couldn't speak very well, but I could understand him. He mumbled, "Move, get out of my way." I complied and he kept wheeling, jerking his arm as he passed. As he continued down the hallway, he almost ran into an older man who was also in a wheelchair.

The older man happened to be blocking his way through no fault of his own. The man who could not sit upright repeated his direction. "Move, get out of my way," he said. The older man looked directly at the first man and said, "No, you are in my hall!" The aggressive man at the 45-degree angle responded, "Move! If you don't get out of my way, I'm going to kill you!"

As I continued to watch this scene, I thought, *You are kidding, how are you going to do that?* The older man retorted, "You'll have to kill me then, because I am not moving!" They proceeded to threaten each other in their barely audible, sickly voices.

The argument continued until a nursing assistant came along and lovingly separated them. These two men were behaving as though they were both five years old. It makes one wonder about the background of these two individuals. Parental influence is so extremely critical. Were they the victims of one sibling being favored over another—possibly missing out on some aspects of their much needed nurturing? What kind of maternal guidance did they have? What could the fathers of these two men have done to strengthen the character of their children? Wise parents find the balance between firmness and affection in disciplining their children.

Some may be wondering if it's possible to keep from having favorites. Yes, by the grace of God, it is definitely possible. It's a decision that is made early that all your children are equally valuable to you, no matter what they do. Look at each one as an individual and consider their strengths as well as their weaknesses. Each one has his or her own set of challenges and talents with potential that must be developed. Most of all, love Christ into them, and bring their gifts out of them. They all need you.

CAN'T I EVEN GO TO THE BATHROOM?

Oh, the sacrifices of motherhood. I remember when my children were young. My oldest child, a daughter, was born a little over a year after my husband and I were married. It took me a total of three months to get pregnant. She wasn't a honeymoon baby, but she was close! Two years later, I had my second child, a son. What a blessing he was! His older sister, who was two at the time, thought it was her responsibility to take care of him. I had a lot of help! Fifteen months later, I delivered another beautiful baby girl. She was the last of the little Buntings.

Taking care of three children in diapers was quite a challenge! I thought that I would never stop changing, feeding, and bathing children—not to mention the endless hours devoted to coloring "masterpieces" with my toddlers. Here's a math problem for you. When three children are potty training, how many times do you have to take them to the bathroom in one day? You lose count around the thirteenth visit, don't you? When food goes in one child, it seems to come out of another.

Everywhere I went, there were three little people with me. Their needs were incessant. Upon leaving restaurants, it looked like a food fight had occurred at our table. No matter where we went, my dinner was cold by the time I got around to it. Every blouse that I owned was stained by a trail of drool. That was because the head of one baby would consistently slide off of the cloth diaper attached to my shoulder as I grabbed one of the other ones who was heading "who knows where." When I was a nursing mom, I got accustomed to walking through the mall with a blanket draped over my shoulder. At that point, who cares?

Yes, that's right, ladies. Motherhood is a joy. It is the joy of loving somebody else more than you love yourself. If you are struggling with the sacrifices of motherhood, I am a living testimony that the old saying practiced at the communion table is true, "This, too will pass."

When you can't use the restroom in peace because somebody knocks on the door and says, "Mommy . . . " When you can't take a bath without someone wanting to come in and put their toy boat in the water with you, when you find out that the stain in your favorite suit won't come out, when you can't get into your own cabinets because of the child locks, remember—this too will pass. The sacrifices that you make now will yield a lifetime of love and blessings.

MOMMY AT HOME: YOU CAN DO IT!

Congratulations! You have decided to be a stay-at-home mom. What a blessing for you to be able to do so. What a mighty hand of influence you will yield for your children. At the same time, it is both an honorable profession and a difficult job that you have chosen.

One of the challenges of being a stay-at-home mom, especially if you came out of the corporate world, is the lack of affirmation. At work someone will tell you when you do a good job. You feel an immediate sense of accomplishment when you complete a project; you know that you have done well. When you carry on a conversation, there are people to talk to who make sense when they talk back. Your work is done with advanced technology and not "little people" toys.

Nobody asks what you did all day, because it is clear. If you hadn't been there, that project wouldn't have been as successful. At home, you don't get a check every two weeks to validate your contribution. Your "check" arrives eighteen years later when God has used you to produce godly children. You see the fruit of your labor when your children demonstrate the values and love for God that you have instilled in them. That is your reward.

If you are choosing to stay at home with your children, ask God to give you a sense of how He views it. You will need to know so that when you open up a magazine and read about other people's successes, your worth won't be diminished while you supervise your children's crayon project. Don't quit because it is hard. Know what God wants for you and be determined to fulfill His will for you. When God directs a mother to be home with her children, He has a reason. And He will enable you to do it. Here are some practical tips for survival.

Invest in Yourself

Because being a stay-at-home mom is such a demanding task, particularly during the preschool period, it is easy to let yourself go. Get up early, take a bath, and get dressed in the morning. It will make you feel better and more productive. Put some makeup on before your husband comes home and comb your hair. He has been looking at attractive women all day. You don't want to look like you've been dragged through the mud (although you may have been—literally).

Even it if takes months to complete it, read a good book during those naptime intervals where you can catch a break. Find one that will be entertaining, informative, or spiritually uplifting. I remember when I was a stay-at-home mom. I was so tired that I could barely read or understand anything. I got one of those children's Bibles from the dollar store. I couldn't concentrate on King James's language, but I could read the kiddy version of the Bible. And read it, I did. I remember standing by the window one day needing so very badly to hear a word from the Lord. I picked up my kiddy Bible and read it voraciously. The words ministered to my spirit in such a powerful way.

You may not be able to do things the "normal" way, but create unique ways in which your needs can be met. In between *Veggie Tales* videos, turn on the news. It airs constantly on some channels. The cadence is good for the children to absorb—it is helpful for developing their thinking and communication skills. And you will be informed when the conversation at dinner doesn't revolve around the children.

Wear Them Out

Before your children are born, you should have a vision for them. That is the reason you are staying home with them—so that you can grow them into the people you envision them to be. Don't waste their time or yours. If you are in the house all day, they are going to wear you out. Children have a lot of energy, and they can easily become bored. If it is just you alone with them, you have to find ways to entertain them. As you develop a daily routine, schedule a time to take them out of the house and let them wear off some energy. Outdoor activities provide entertainment and assist in their growth process.

If you live in a metropolitan area, it is easy to let them exhaust themselves. Get them up in the morning, bathe them, and feed them breakfast. The process can be time consuming as well as challenging. But when you finish and load them into the car, the hard part is pretty much over. They are going somewhere, and to little ones, anywhere is an adventure. You can take them to a friend's house, and they can play while you visit. You can take them to the park, to the museum, to a church function, to the library, or to a mini-golf course.

Try a pizza place for variety. Many fast food restaurants have play areas. Morning skating sessions are very inexpensive, and the dollar movies also provide a nice break. Be creative. There is always somewhere you can take them where they can learn something, and you can watch them learn it. Fabric and food stores often have demonstrations. At the very least, warehouse food stores often have free food samples. If you keep the little ones in the cart, they can't run, but they get to look around. Take your time, and don't rush; you don't have to be home until afternoon. Farms often have free rides during certain seasons, and the farmer's market is just plain fun.

Coupon books offer a great advantage because they include ideas and ways that you can save money. We used to buy two big coupon books that contained buy-one-get-one free coupons. In the morning, I would look in the coupon book and pick somewhere to go. You may be a better planner than I was. But the idea is the same. Find somewhere to go and take them out. Don't return home until about 2:00 p.m. By that time they are worn out and ready for a snack. It will be easier to persuade them to watch a video or take a nap.

There are plenty of opportunities for them to be entertained; you can also check the Internet and local newspapers. Festivals are good, even if you have to drive for a while. Keep some car games in the trunk or the back of your SUV, along with a cooler containing water and juice. When they are drinking, they are not talking. Flower festivals, fall festivals, art festivals, music festivals, any kind of festival will do.

Drop by the local grocery store on the way and let them pick their food for lunch. Of course, when you have two toddlers you need one of those double strollers. Just deal with the inconvenience and keep your focus on long-term benefits. We used to do one fruit, one drink,

one chip, one sweet, and one sandwich. Then you can find a table at
the festival and not have to spend any money. If you have extra money,
though, an ice cream cone goes a long way.

As they get a little older, vacation Bible school (VBS) hopping in
the summer is great. You can take them in the morning, let them
learn about Christ until about noon, and then pick up your happy children. Then if you can take them rollerskating in the afternoon, before
you know it, the day is over. Sometimes you can get in two VBS programs in one day. This is how you do it:

Drive around your town toward the beginning of the summer.
Most churches advertise their VBS dates on their billboard. Mark the
dates on a calendar; they usually last a week. On the first morning of
the VBS, register your children. Of course, the children will have to
get up early, and you'll have to get them ready. But they will be excited
because VBS is fun.

It doesn't matter if the church is large or small—most VBS programs are well worth the effort. You can stick around and talk to other
moms or run errands. It is a good idea to stay the first day, though, to
evaluate the quality. If the children come home and didn't have a
good time, try the next one on the schedule that you created.

City park and recreation programs are usually jam-packed with children's activities. Sign up your children for the ones that may be of interest. If for some reason they miss a day, the sky isn't going to fall. You can
usually find something else they want to do. Some classes are free.

You can also contact the cultural arts department in your city's
administrative office. There are often free camps for children to develop
their acting, painting, and artistic skills over the summer. Watch out
for relationships the children might develop and pay close attention
to the kind of influence other children may have. You are raising godly
children, and little ones pick up habits quickly. Otherwise, they might
enjoy a dance class!

As the children get older, check your local colleges. Many of them
have educational programs for children during the summer months.
Monitor the program to make sure that they're not teaching any

theory that contradicts Scripture. You don't want the children to pick up something you have to undo.

Summer swimming is also a great pastime. Some children want to swim every day. A two-hour swimming class is both physically beneficial and stimulating. In addition, if you live in a metropolitan area that has a Public Broadcasting Station, make sure you tune into their annual or semiannual auction. You might be the only bidder for that special deal. One year, I picked up a three-month gymnastics class membership at a local gymnasium for only ten dollars. It lasted the whole summer, and the children loved their little class!

When you're spending time at home, using the educational workbooks you can pick up at any grocery or drug store will work you a little more, but they give the children an advantage at school. If you assign a certain number of pages a day, you'll be surprised at how much they learn. One summer, my son advanced a whole grade level because of the work that we did in those books.

Finally, let the children develop their creativity with craft projects. Popsicle sticks fascinate kids; particularly when you combine them with glue, construction paper, and a variety of objects you find in your junk drawer. What child doesn't like making puppets out of socks or playing games? If you make up the games, you don't have to pay for them. There are always simple party game books at bookstores that you can modify for your children.

Engaging your children in productive activity is what makes being a stay-at-home mom work to the greatest potential. And remember, every moment is a teaching moment. You will be pleased to know how easy it is to teach your children God's Word when you show them how it relates to their everyday experiences.

Yes, this sounds like a full-time job, doesn't it? It takes a lot of time, stamina, and brainpower to be the mother that God created you to be. But, as you co-labor with Him, God will enable you and empower you to do your job well. He will also give you common sense. If the children are tired or not feeling well on occasion, let them stay home and play. Don't drive them; develop them.

Get Rid of Your Expectations

It would serve you well to remember this important aspect of your marital relationship. After a day of working with your children, don't expect your husband to meet all your needs when he gets home from work. If he comes home and asks the question, "What did you do all day?" don't get mad. He doesn't understand, and he probably never will.

The best that he can do is take you out to dinner from time to time and find other ways to let you know how special you are. But trying to explain your role in a manner that he will respond to with all the right words—all the time—is a long shot. The bottom line is to look for validation from heaven, and serve your husband. You will reap far greater rewards, and it will keep you from having false expectations about what your husband can and cannot provide for you.

The Five-Minute Cleanup

It's a job to stay on top of, but try not to keep your house in a constant state of messiness. Then again, don't try to have the whole house spotless either—you'll be miserable. At the least, make sure the front room is straight. And make an effort to straighten up before your husband comes home.

The five-minute cleanup will work great in a hurry. Set the egg timer and tell the kids, "We're going to clean up this room in five minutes. Ready, set, go!" Then let everybody run around and pick up stuff. At the end of five minutes, go to the next room and repeat the process. This will bring some order to the major rooms in the house.

Put dinner in the Crock-Pot before you leave home in the morning. That way, you don't have a lot of dishes to clean up, and you don't have to figure out what to do for dinner at the last minute. If you have additional cleaning to do around the house, you can finish up when the children are asleep. That way they won't have an opportunity to mess it back up so quickly.

A Time for Worship

It is extremely important that you do not neglect your spiritual life. You will need the Lord's grace to keep you going when it gets rough. Therefore, finding time to worship God is essential. In worship you can relax. You can express to the Lord how much you love Him. Tell Him about your gratitude, your pain, and your desires. His presence will be calming, soothing, and encouraging. When you offer up the work that you are doing as a stay-at-home mother, God will be pleased with your labor of love. After all, you are doing this for His glory.

You are going to need to know that He is satisfied with you, because there will be times when nobody else is. Little children don't always show the most appreciative behavior. Therefore, the security of your relationship with God will keep you from having second thoughts about the sacrifice you are making.

It is human nature to think that the proverbial "other side of the fence" is more appealing. Even if you think that the workplace would bring more immediate satisfaction, the time that you invest in your children will bring far greater rewards in the long term.

One more thing, do not forget the necessity of participating in corporate worship. When you are in a congregation of worshipers, you can receive words of encouragement and support that you cannot get when you're home alone with the children. More than likely there will be other women who are having a similar experience, and you can share some of your struggles with each other.

Finding the time and space to worship at home is nearly impossible; your worship can be interrupted any minute by the summons, "Mommy . . ." When you can place the children in nursery care during service, it will allow you to get in your worship zone and spend some time focusing on God alone.

Taxi, Anyone? Using Your Time Well

Take it from me—there may be times in your life when you feel like you live in the car. You take the children to school and pick them up from school. You take them to their friends' houses, to and from church activities, and to extracurricular school activities. On Saturdays, you hurry from one destination to another, picking this one up, dropping another one off.

I was riding behind a family van yesterday that looked immaculate. On the back window was a sticker that read, "Mother on the Edge." It accurately described the kind of experience I am referring to, and I understood the message completely. There went another dedicated mother doing all that she could to take care of her children.

By the time everybody gets in the car all sweaty, tired, and excited, it's easy to just turn on the radio and let them argue until you get home. Don't do it. You have a captive audience during the drive home. Your car time is probably your most valuable time to communicate with your children and help them understand your expectations. It is equally important to ask them questions and listen to them talk as well.

I love the Socratic method of teaching. Socrates was a renowned philosopher who lived in Greece many years before Christ was born. Instead of presenting information, he would spend his day in the public square asking questions. His questions would guide the responder to a startling conclusion: they didn't know as much as they thought they knew.

The ancient theologian Saint Augustine, a father of the Christian church, also used the Socratic method to instruct his son. If it was good enough for them, it's good enough for me. Whenever I wanted to guide my children to a specific conclusion, I would ask them insightful questions that made them think. It was a perfect scenario—they were thinking and I was in control.

Somewhere in the midst of the conversation, I would talk about what the Bible said about the matter we were discussing. As a result, they learned to evaluate their behavior by the Word of God, even if they didn't always follow what they knew to be right. I knew that I couldn't make them always do right, but I could definitely teach them right from wrong. And I used my car time to do it.

In essence, the time that you spend with your children is priceless. They are forming opinions, and the opinions they form will reap consequences that you will have to deal with later on. It is in your best interest to capture all the time you can get in their developmental years—and use it to teach them.

Moreover, for those who work outside of the home, this car time is even more valuable. When they come home from school, it will be homework time, and moral instruction will often yield to mathematic calculations. An opportunity for quality time occurs right when they get out of school. When you pick them up, they are ready to talk. During the drive home, put down the cell phone and listen. It will be the best half-hour you will spend with them. And that half-hour of quality time every day can change their lives—and yours.

In fact, your cell phone can be the enemy of intimacy with your children. When you are at home, be at home. When you are at work, be at work. Devote yourself to the task before you at any given moment. That way, you maximize who you are in every context. If you take care of your children when you are with them, you don't have to feel guilty when you are not with them. If you take care of the office when you are there, you don't have to feel bad when you say, "Now, it's time for my family."

However, if your employer doesn't want you to spend time with your family, that's the wrong employer for you. Most organizations will take everything they can get—and then some. Don't give them your children's lives. Also, if you own your own business, remember it is God's business. If you take time off and play with your children, you are not cheating your business. God will bless your business as He chooses. Fulfill all the work you can in the time that you have to do it. But don't let the business destroy your home.

TEENAGE TERRORS

It's a well-established fact that the teenage years can be very difficult. At this point, children suddenly become experts on any given subject and tend to act as though they know more than you do. They may think that they're grown, but they are not. In biblical days, part of the culture was for children to be married in their early teens. That was all right for the time; it was an expectation that people were prepared for and a norm that children were groomed to practice.

However, today that is not the standard that we live by. We do not expect or want our young people to get married at an early age. They are not ready to handle the responsibilities of marriage. So then, while they are under our care, the question becomes, how do we survive until they mature into adulthood? Scripture clearly lays out rules about how teenagers are to behave. It is up to us to enforce these guidelines in our homes.

R-E-S-P-E-C-T

"Children, obey your parents in the Lord, for this is right, Honor your father and mother (which is the first commandment with a promise), so that it may be well with you, and that you may live long on the earth." (Ephesians 6:1–3)

The children that we bring into this world rightfully live under our care. In return, parents are supposed to receive respect from their children. One of the very first Scripture passages that you should teach your children is this one. We pay the bills and assume accountability for our offspring—we reserve the right to be obeyed.

Furthermore, a major aspect of obedience is respect. But this is a learned behavior, and children must understand that they are to give you respect. You must introduce them to the Word of God and explain that God has certain rules for them to follow in obedience to the rules that we set. We are the boss; we are in control. It is up to us to teach our children what is required of them. If they don't learn from us, how can we suppose that they should know?

The passage in Ephesians chapter 6 is based on the Ten Commandments (Deuteronomy 5:16). It is a very serious offense to God when we don't get this right. In fact, this is the only commandment that God attached a promise along with it. As a result, believers are expected to make sure that children obey the rules that their parents establish. When your children have received the proper education on this principle, tell them that God promises them a special blessing when they obey it. They will live long and prosperous lives just because they gave their mother and father the proper respect.

Otherwise, when you fail to apply the proper discipline and allow your children to disobey you without consequences, God is not pleased. It is not His desire for parents to be ruled by their children, but that is a dangerous outcome that results as a lack of following God's commandment. When children show disrespect, they violate God's order for the home, and chaos ensues. It is up to the parents, the adults, to enforce their rules and ensure that the home is a peaceful environment. For us to tolerate anything less is to dishonor God—and that is something no one wants to be found guilty of doing.

TEACH THE WORD

"Train up a child in the way he should go, even when he is old he will not depart from it." (Proverbs 22:6)

From a very young age, it is time to maximize your influence by training your children to love the Lord. Begin by demonstrating how they should apply the Word in their daily lives. When they are confronted by a situation at school, try asking, "What does God say about this?" Point out the verses of Scripture that are applicable and talk them through it until they reach an understanding. You may have to repeat the same process until they can explain back to you what you are trying to convey.

As they grow older and are having difficulty, continue to build on the process you began when they were younger. Guide them in using a Bible with a concordance or a Bible promise book (this is a book that contains specific subjects and Scriptures that relate to those areas). The Bible speaks on all topics, including: friendship, dating, parents, worry, love, forgiveness, and so on. Show them how to pull out the principles of God's Word and relate them to their situations. Also encourage them to write out their thoughts, expressing to God their struggles and triumphs.

At some point, they will be out of your sight. Even then, the Word that has been planted in them will guide them or convict them. You will have to trust that the truth of God's Word has taken root in their hearts and they will follow the example you have laid out for them.

SURVIVOR: FINALLY CALLED BLESSED

"Her children rise up and bless her; her husband also, and he praises her." (Proverbs 31:28)

You ask the question, is it worth it? The answer is a resounding, Yes! My children are grown now; and surprise, they love me! I am a witness to the truth of God's Word. I am not telling you about something that I haven't already lived through. After all the discipline, guiding, directing, and demanding, they can't wait to see me when they come home to visit. After the frustration and irritation, the cleaning and cooking, the washing and folding, the curfews, the homework, the car privileges being given and mommy-stalker following them to see what they were *really* doing—they say thanks!

I say to all of that, it's about time. I am just writing to encourage you. It does pay off in the end. As a testament to your work of love, they will grow up and call you blessed! And, believe me, what a blessing it will be.

CREATE A LEGACY

"Grandchildren are the crown of old men, and the glory of sons is their father." (Proverbs 17:6)

Your children will most likely be around long after you are gone. You may be blessed to have grandchildren. The Word of God commands us to instruct our children and our grandchildren in God's ways and laws (Deuteronomy 4:9). If you have accomplished your goal of teaching your children to live well, they will carry your legacy forward. By creating a strong bond of family ties, it will go on for generations to come.

As you firmly direct them with mutual respect, when they grow older they will learn to appreciate your guidance. Don't be afraid to continue to direct them in their decisions. The more they see that you are right, the more they will value your wisdom.

But remember that this kind of trust only comes from what you have instilled in them from an early age. One of the most important things you can do for your children is to pray for them every day. God is your partner in raising your children to be godly individuals; you can trust that He will answer your righteous prayers. He will be your guiding light to lead you and your children to victory.

USING YOUR DIVINE DESIGN

You are uniquely gifted to mother your children. Use everything at your disposal to practice kingdom-building motherhood. It takes all that you have, but if you put your brainpower, your willpower, your prayer power, your fasting, your heart, and some godly discipline into it, you can do it. You can be the mother that your children need—according to your divine design.

Chapter 7

What to Do in the Midst of a Dilemma

At the very time I was writing this book, I was sitting in the emergency room. It was the third time that particular month. I am all too familiar with emergency rooms. With three active children, we practically lived in them. One of them was always getting hurt while playing sports or getting injured in some other way. But I never really expected this. I suppose that I thought my mother would be well forever. But she's not, and I'm first in line to take care of her.

FIRST IN LINE

It is difficult to care for an aging parent. There are so many decisions to be made. And there is so much to find out; so many preparations to be made. Do you have a medical power of attorney, or do you have to process a guardianship? How much money do they have? Do they have long-term care insurance? What about a "do not resuscitate" order? Are they eligible for Medicare or Medicaid? What exactly is Medicare

Part D? You never had to know all of this until they got so sick.

And then there are the emotions. Tears come from nowhere when you remember better days, grieving the loss that they don't even know they are experiencing. You watch helplessly, knowing that for your loved one, the days ahead on earth are probably not better than what they have already experienced. Their destiny is heaven, but you just don't want them to go right now. Caring for them is a joy and a drain. You wish you had more to give, but you don't. After all, you still have a family to care for. You have your own children, your husband, and your job. You don't want to lose contact with your friends, but you have so little time for social interaction.

There are bright spots, particularly when your parents are mentally alert. They can go to the mall with you or to church and enjoy being around other people. On the other hand, they can do strange things such as take their medications improperly, insist on having their way even when their request is not rational or convenient, or talk about having boyfriends or girlfriends way past the age where that seems to be reasonable or appropriate. If you happen to spend time in a nursing home, you will find out how curious that community of elderly people can be!

When an elderly parent lives in your home, it generates an incessant amount of work. You want to do it, because you love them. But work it is just the same. Turning them to prevent bedsores, constantly feeding them, giving them their medications, and attending to their personal hygiene can be an overwhelming task. Even when they are not bedridden, they require a lot of attention. And they aren't always so pleasant, either. They know that they brought you into this world, and there are days when they may not feel like doing what you tell them.

At the same time, there are so many other demands on us. Our children are often still in our homes or in our pockets. Many times they are attending college and call for help or advice on graduate school applications, tests, papers, or life in general. Even after college they come back home.

Moreover, sometimes our children have children and need our

help. Married couples move back home to relieve financial strain and save money. I remember when I was growing up. I didn't want to move back home! But this is a new generation, and I understand that there are such things as economic factors that cannot be ignored. Most of all, our children like us so much that they don't mind living with us. What it comes down to is that we don't get a break.

YOU'RE THE MOM

One day a little boy and his mother were riding a carousel. He chose to ride one of the horses, and his mom had taken one of the benches. As his horse went up and down, he began to get dizzy. Determined to be a big boy, he closed his eyes and prayed. "God, please don't let me get sick. I don't want anybody to know that I'm dizzy." The carousel went round and round and the horse continued to go up and down. Soon the boy began to get sleepy. He got sleepier and sleepier, and his body began to slump.

Noticing her son's unusual position, his mother arose from her seat and went over to the horse. Touching him, she asked, "Son, is everything all right?" He straightened up and opened his eyes, still determined not to appear sick. But his mom knew him. She invited him to come and sit beside her because *she* wasn't feeling well. Because he wanted to take care of his mom, he dismounted proudly and took a seat beside her on the bench. He had wanted to get off of the horse, but he didn't want to make a scene. Now he didn't have to. He had been rescued by his mother's love.

For many of us, our roles have reversed. We have watched our parents ride the carousel of life, and for a long time they were doing just fine. But then they began to be sick. They didn't want anyone to know and simply prayed for God's deliverance. Finally, they could not function alone anymore. When we noticed, we approached them to save their pride. "Mother, we have an extra room and could use some help with the children. Why don't you come and live with us?" Or, "Dad, why don't you move to Chicago; it would be so nice to have you closer."

Perhaps you said, "Mom, why don't you let me just bring over dinner from now on? It's too much trouble for you to try and cook every day." Or you might have suggested, "Dad, why don't you call me when you need to go somewhere? I'll drive you. Something seems to be going on with your car." For a time they tried to straighten up because they didn't want to appear sick. Finally, they agreed, and we provided a dignified exit from the carousel of their life. Congratulations, if this was similar to your experience—you are to be commended.

STOP! HELP!

"My grace is sufficient for you, for power is perfected in weakness. Most gladly, therefore, I will rather boast about my weaknesses, so that the power of Christ may dwell in me." (2 Corinthians 12:9)

Some of you are in seemingly impossible circumstances right now. Maybe you have grown children that are still dependents. Maybe your child is in trouble. Maybe a parent is very ill, and you are the one designated to care for him or her. Maybe you are personally ill. I have good news for you. It is possible to know that you are being stretched, but at the same time you don't feel the pain of being stretched. God will show you what He can do when you trust Him. This is between you and Him; nobody else has to understand.

This was something that the apostle Paul had to deal with. He found himself in a difficult situation and just wanted the Lord to make it all go away. Paul was a faithful servant of the Lord, but he had a problem in his life. And he took it to God. He and the Lord had a great relationship, so whenever he prayed, the Lord heard him and responded. But that didn't happen this particular time, and he prayed again and again. It was unusual for him to ask twice, but three times?

What did he do wrong? Was God displeased with him for some reason? He had enough faith; he had traveled all over the world planting churches and trusting God with his life in all kinds of dangerous situations.

When God finally answered Paul, He did not do what Paul asked of Him. Instead, this was God's response recorded in 2 Corinthians 12:9, *"My grace is sufficient for you."* God did answer Paul's cry, but not in the way that Paul wanted Him to. When you cry out to God, He will answer your prayer too. But that doesn't mean that you'll get what you want. What it does mean is that God will help you to endure. By giving you His grace, He will respond to your need and give you a peace and ability to handle that which you never thought you would have to handle.

God's grace can do that for you. He makes the unbearable bearable. Sometimes God will bring people along that will help you. Other times, He chooses to strengthen you in the midst of your circumstance. Either way, you will know that He is answering your cry. When I was growing up and fell into challenging circumstances, there was a phrase my father frequently used. He would say, "Handle it." That was the beginning and the end of the sentence. It was simultaneously an expectation, a command, and an exhortation.

Recently on a Wednesday night at church, I was crying out to the Lord as I struggled with my mother's dementia. This was a particularly difficult night. All day long I had been recalling what Mother used to be like—how alive she used to be. Now she was on medication that made her sleep most of the time. God heard my cry. In the middle of my pastor's prayer, I heard him speak the words, "Handle it." I almost could not believe my own ears. Then he said it again, "Handle it." I have no clue in what context he was using that phrase, but that was the Holy Spirit's voice to me.

Suddenly, I was okay. I received the strength to do what was necessary. I could handle it. God doesn't always change the circumstances, but He will give you the ability to "handle it."

Another word for grace is "favor." When life brings challenges, know that you are still God's child. The favor that He provides is strong enough for you to not only endure, but to also be victorious in the midst of your circumstances. Listen to Him and allow Him to direct you. Without God's help, there is no way possible for you to know what to do with your parents, what to do with your children, your husband, your job, and other responsibilities.

This is an urgent necessity. You need Him now. If you call on Him, His favor will be sufficient for you. What does His favor mean to you? It means that you can do it. It means that He will bear you up physically and emotionally.

DECISION TIME

If you don't know what to do in the middle of a dilemma—ask God. He won't get tired of your asking, like other people might do. After a while they want you to quit whining. They don't really know anyway. But God doesn't get tired of your asking. He delights in it. When you ask, He will give you wisdom about what you should do. Follow His wisdom to freedom. As you strengthen your relationship with Him, you won't need affirmation from men about your decisions.

Some time ago, Mother was in the hospital. After the procedure that she needed was complete, she would not wake up. As a result, she could not eat. The physicians were not sure if she would ever wake up. About two weeks later, the doctor recommended a feeding tube. I prayed diligently, because I did not want to make a mistake. I had heard how many people become incapacitated after a feeding tube is inserted. Finally, I agreed, and signed the paperwork. The tube would be inserted the next day. Mother was still asleep, and I left to prepare for an early morning meeting.

One of her previous nurses happened to go by the hospital to visit her. She was a kind and compassionate woman and felt it was her calling to care for older, sick people. She called me from the hospital, and we discussed what was about to happen. She said, "Karia, think about her quality of life. I cannot tell you what to do, but she hasn't awakened from the previous anesthesia. How do you think her body will handle more?"

She was an answer to my prayer. I got up, went to that hospital, and negated my previous authorizations. Then I went in to talk to my mother who was still unconscious. "Mom," I said. "You are a fighter. It is time for you to fight. I am not going to put a feeding tube in you. You need to live, so fight your way back." Somehow I had a quiet peace about my decision.

Two days later Mother came back as strong as ever. She opened her eyes and looked at the clock. "It is three o'clock, I have somewhere I need to go!" she said. She proceeded to start laughing and talking to everyone. The nurses were shocked. One of them said, "I can't believe this!" They all commented on the fact that she had awakened. They never expected it.

Even when you don't know what to do and could perhaps make the wrong decision, God can intervene. I am convinced that He has my mother's days in His hands, and she will be around as long as He wants her here. After that, she will be with Him. Whatever happens, I know that God's grace will be sufficient for me to handle it.

FINDING COMFORT IN HIM

Paul went on to explain that *"power is perfected in weakness."* The root of the word "weakness" is the same as that used for the English word "anesthesia." God says that His strength is the strongest when you are under anesthesia. When you can't do it, God can. When life has knocked you out cold, that's when God is at His best in your life. He is supplying your emotional needs in ways you could not dream possible. He is undergirding you. His strength is showing through, and people wonder how in the world you are holding up so well.

Sometimes life can be so difficult that you can no longer do anything for yourself; yet, you can depend on God. Go ahead, give up. Get on your knees in the morning and say, "God, I can't handle today. I don't know what to do today. I just want to rest in You. Lord, You make the decisions today. Guide me by Your Holy Spirit."

Then get up, read the Word, and listen for His answer. Focus on the Lord for the rest of the day. Rest in Him and do what He says. You will be amazed by the fact that His Spirit will guide you as the day goes on. You will feel a sense of peace while He directs. By His grace, you get everything done that needs to be done. That's how His strength is made perfect when you are weak and depending on Him.

But if you say, "I don't hear Him. He doesn't direct me." I would tell you to draw closer, watch, and listen. Sometimes He allows difficult circumstances in our lives just to get us to the point where we listen better. When He relieves the circumstances, we're left with a better prayer life.

Paul says the results are worth the journey. He understood that it was God's grace that he needed more than anything else. That made him able to confess, *"Most gladly, therefore, I will rather boast about my weaknesses, so that the power of Christ may dwell in me"* (2 Corinthians 12:9). He found out how wonderful it is to be under the anesthesia of God's grace. He found out that he had more power when he was unable to function in His own strength. That is because God substitutes His strength at times when we need it. And God's strength is far superior to our own strength. That's when we have the most impact!

There is a spiritual purpose for what you are going through. In the midst of it you can find comfort in the loving arms of God. Paul described it this way, *"I can do all things through [Christ] who strengthens me"* (Philippians 4:13). Besides this, the apostle James says that we should count everything that comes our way as joy—even our tests and trials (see James 1:2).

Give it a try. Decide all this is joy for you, and you will reap the reward of your faith in God. When your faith is put to the test, you also learn the art of endurance. It may not always feel so good, but God will assure you that He is in control and will not allow anything to ultimately destroy you. Go ahead, press on and trust God; He will never leave you or forsake you.

NURTURING YOUR DIVINE DESIGN

Give God your body during your trials. Your body is not your own, so you have no right to wear it out. If you are a caretaker for someone, don't forget to first take care of yourself. If that is what God has called you to be, then do it to His glory. But if He has not, don't attempt to take on this great responsibility. Do what He has for you to do at this time in your life, and not what people expect you to do. Whatever you do, make sure you hear from God—and obey Him.

Even when you are facing challenges, God wants this to be a wonderful time of growth for you. Take time to nurture yourself. Give yourself permission to go on a vacation, get a spa treatment, or simply take a few days off. You were born for such a time as this. Walk in faith, knowing that God has prepared everything for you to live your life rich in His care—no matter what experiences you have to endure.

Finally Friends: *The Importance of Relationships*

he angel of the Lord spoke to Mary, the mother of Jesus, and said, *"Greetings, favored one! The Lord is with you"* (Luke 1:28).

In that moment, everything changed. Mary had once been only a young girl, bright-eyed and in great anticipation of her upcoming wedding. She had fantasized about each detail and celebrated the cheerful rituals of engagement. It seemed that everyone shared in her glee. Mary was a virtuous girl. She had followed the ordinances of the Torah and had remained a respectable young woman of honor and purity.

Suddenly, her life was interrupted. The angel proclaimed that the Holy Spirit would overshadow her and that she would be with child. Mary was perplexed as her mind raced and her heart pounded in her chest. One can only imagine what she must have been thinking: *My son will be the greatest man who has ever lived! Who would have believed that I would bear the Son of God? What an honor! What will Joseph do? What will the village think? How do I explain this? No one will believe me, I am a disgrace. The Son of God . . . that was what the Spirit of the Lord said to me. Joseph will be so hurt. Will he even believe me? Lord, I pray that he will believe me. Please let him believe me. They will want to stone me for committing adultery. He will never want to marry me. Lord, me? Are You sure? I should be the one to raise the Son of God? How is this possible, Lord? I am not worthy.*

Mary decided to leave the village; she knew who to turn to. She would visit her cousin. Elizabeth knew her; she would believe her story. Mary could share her life, her experience, her calling, and Elizabeth would understand. The angel had told Mary that her cousin was also with child. She could hardly wait to see her and hurried quickly to Elizabeth's house. But when she arrived, there was no need for Mary to give her the news. At Mary's greeting, Elizabeth's baby leaped inside of her.

Immediately Elizabeth was filled with the Holy Spirit and proclaimed a joyful declaration! In a loud voice, she pronounced, *"Blessed are you among women, and blessed is the fruit of your womb"* (Luke 1:42). Then Elizabeth continued with a great testament to what God had done, *"And how has it happened to me, that the mother of my Lord would come to me? For behold, when the sound of your greeting reached my ears, the baby leaped in my womb for joy. And blessed is she who believed that there would be a fulfillment of what had been spoken to her by the Lord"* (Luke 1:43–45).

Amazing. Mary was glad to be with her cousin, her friend. Here was someone who understood. Elizabeth would celebrate with her. She would smile and dance and shout, even in this strange situation. Elizabeth would not question her, be cynical, or try to intimidate her. So, dance and rejoice they did! The two cousins glorified the Lord for their two miracle babies! By the time she left, Mary was comfortable, comforted, and prepared for what lay ahead.

Have you ever been in a strange situation and just wanted someone to share it with? Sometimes you need a friend. You want someone trustworthy who can identify with your joys and struggles. The problem is that we are so busy that we often don't have time to develop these kinds of relationships. Then when trouble comes, we feel alone, abandoned, and sad.

Even Mary, the mother of Jesus, needed a friend. You and I do as well. God, in His gracious plan, did not expect for us to go through life alone. Let's follow Mary's example and find someone reliable with whom we can share. We will have a more enjoyable and fulfilled life.

WOMAN TO WOMAN

If Mary had not already cultivated a friendship with her cousin, she wouldn't have had anyone to visit at a time when she needed someone to confide in the most. Elizabeth's house was a safe haven, away from prying eyes and nosy people. Both women were committed to God. Both of them were spiritual. They were a perfect match.

The Lord has given me wonderful friends whom I love. As a nerd in grade school, a career-oriented young woman, married and busy in grad school, and later a full-time mom pursuing a doctorate, I chose to delay developing intimate personal relationships. Although early in my career I had been outgoing and fun, old business and social acquaintances seemed to vanish as I engrossed myself in the rigors of study and life.

After my family started a business, time was even more limited. I lived in virtual isolation as my husband and I worked long hours to make our business successful. I found myself drained and lonely, longing for female companionship. Without affirmation and people with whom I could share my life, I became insecure.

I began to think that I was really a boring person. I didn't know why anyone would even want to talk with me. Theology, humanity, art, history, and literature were all I thought about. *Who else is thinking about this kind of thing?* I wondered. Moreover, popular culture didn't interest me much. I knew little to nothing about what Brad Pitt or Beyonce was doing and didn't have time to care. I had gradually become a quiet and introverted person with no friends in sight.

Then one day I found myself volunteering at a Christian conference and met up with an old friend. We started having a great conversation! She actually liked me, and I couldn't believe it. She was interested in the same things that I was, and she talked my language. I was so amazed. She and I had a discussion about Abraham's learning style, and then we talked about Paul's learning style.

I was so pleasantly surprised! It was hard to believe that anybody was interested in this kind of thing other than me. We developed a wonderful friendship, and I cannot tell you what that has meant to me. Even as I write, tears come to my eyes. Her presence in my life has made an amazing difference.

If you are not one to have close relationships; I hope that you will find someone with whom you can build a lasting friendship. When you are lonely, a good friend can pick you up. A friend will bring out the best in you and make you feel like it is OK for you to just be you. God never wanted you to go through life without the companionship of a close friend. It is part of His divine design for you to have one.

In the book of Philippians, Paul spoke God's mind. He wrote about how to act in order to have genuine friendships. He began by saying, *"Therefore if there is any encouragement in Christ, if there is any consolation of love, if there is any fellowship of the Spirit, if any affection and compassion, make my joy complete by being of the same mind, maintaining the same love, united in spirit, intent on one purpose"* (Philippians 2:1–2).

Paul was in jail as he penned these survival instructions to the church at Philippi. They were terrified because their enemies were out to get them. He urged them to develop real, deep, sacrificial relationships with one another. The Holy Spirit can also help you and me to develop meaningful, intimate friendships that can last through the years.

God's Word reflects my sentiment completely. The relationship between Mary and Elizabeth is also revealed here. And I know that having a friend in my life with whom to share a mutual understanding of life's purpose is truly a blessing from God. If you already hold such relationships, know that you are a blessed woman. For those who have yet to discover someone who is likeminded, I say keep looking. God will place a friend in your life just when you need her most.

CONSOLATION IN CHRIST

Scripture teaches us about the kind of enriching relationship that we can have with the Lord. In turn, everything that we learn we are to apply to the relationships that we develop with our sisters in Christ. As He imparts more knowledge to us, we can share it with one another. This is the way to build up each other and strengthen the bond of friendship.

I believe that is why Paul wrote the following, *"Blessed be the God and Father of our Lord Jesus Christ, the Father of mercies and God of all comfort, who comforts us in all our affliction so that we will be able to comfort those who are in any affliction with the comfort with which we ourselves are comforted by God"* (2 Corinthians 1:3–4).

The first consolation you are assured of in difficult times is your identity in Christ. When things get rough, remember you are a child of the Most High God. He has made it so that ultimately you are going to win. No matter what is happening in your life, you are already victorious because God says so. It's no wonder that we can say, *"Thanks be to God, who always leads us in triumph in Christ, and manifests through us the sweet aroma of the knowledge of Him in every place"* (2 Corinthians 2:14). God is pleased when we send up the wonderful fragrance that emanates from our efforts to carry His words of life everywhere that we go. As we bless others, we are blessed.

The second consolation is worship. In worship, you experience God's presence. You know in your heart that your magnificent God will do what He said He would do for you. The third consolation in Christ is in the Word. The Bible is full of promises to you, and if you will hear them, you can be assured that God has it all worked out. By faith, you can thank Him for answering your prayers. In common vernacular, we say, "It's already all right." Sometimes when you are in a crisis, it takes strong faith to believe that God has the solution. He does. And you can find consolation in Him.

COMFORT IN LOVE

When trouble comes our way, we can hold on to God's Word and confess, *"But in all these things we overwhelmingly conquer through Him who loved us"* (Romans 8:37). When Paul wrote, *"If there is any consolation of love,"* the image of consolation is not simply referring to the comfort of a gentle hug and a warm glass of milk. It speaks of the kind of comfort that includes encouragement and inspiration that you need when going through hard times.

This is the type of comfort you experience when you spend time with family and friends who love and support you. You leave their presence feeling stimulated and refreshed. It is this kind of comfort that you receive from expressions of genuine love.

I had three children in college at one time. When they became stressed, tired, frustrated, and worn out—they came home. In my household, there was always something going on. My husband is a shaker and mover, and my house was always shaking and moving! When the children arrived, they would enjoy a weekend of good, plain old family fun. Hanging out with their old friends, eating barbeque and hot dogs, and watching movies until the wee hours of the morning inevitably refreshed them. They went back to school with renewed energy and focus.

The first year my son was in college, he came home almost every weekend. His college was two and a half hours away, so it wasn't a long drive for him. My husband would talk to him and say, "Son, why don't you stay at school some weekends?" He would say, "Okay," but the next weekend he would be back at home again! Home was where my children received the comfort of love that they needed to see them through.

From where do you get your comfort of love? It seems difficult to work a social life into our busy schedules. Just visiting friends on a Sunday afternoon takes effort. But our lack of relationship with other believers makes life more difficult for us. Even if you are married, your husband can't meet all your companionship needs, and you can't meet all of his. You are a part of a body of believers that is designed to be your extended family. Take a break this week and invite someone to lunch for a time of fellowship and encouragement.

When Mary visited her cousin, she experienced the stimulating force of sharing time with another believing woman. What a wonderful companion Mary must have been to the older woman, Elizabeth, as she anticipated her first child. They probably had quite a visit and a lively conversation. Elizabeth may have asked Mary, "Do you think I will be a good mother?" Or, she may have expressed her concern, by saying, "I can't imagine running after a little baby!" Mary would have affirmed, by saying, "Of course, you'll be wonderful!"

As they fetched water or washed clothes together, they probably mused over the color of their babies' eyes and praised God for His goodness. Both women were stimulated and encouraged to be the best mothers they could be. They experienced the fellowship of love. That's what God wants for you. Isn't it what you want for yourself?

FELLOWSHIP OF THE SPIRIT: AFFECTION AND COMPASSION

You and I can rest in the fellowship we have with our Lord. We can rejoice in our relationship with Him. When Paul wrote, *"If there is any fellowship of the Spirit,"* he was saying that we need to rely on close associations with the Holy Spirit and with other believers. Have you ever been to a conference and sat beside someone you didn't know, only to talk almost all the way through the conference? Wasn't that fun? It feels good to share your life with someone who shares your values.

I lead a Bible study at Oak Cliff Bible Fellowship. Full of budding and mature friendships, it is a blessing to me. We meet from 9:30 a.m. to 12:30 p.m. every Tuesday. There is a corresponding "Mother's Day Out" program in which the children can remain until 3:00 p.m. Over the course of a year, more and more women stay after Bible study for meaningful discussions. There are women of all life stages: younger and more mature, mothers and seniors alike who stay until the end, sharing their lives with one another.

One day, one of the participants came into the gym where the Bible study is held just as we were wrapping up the session. She had to work that day, but when she saw several tables of women still sitting and talking she exclaimed, "I knew someone would still be here!" She pulled up a chair and joined in the conversation. She needed affection, compassion, and fellowship and knew where to find it.

In these intimate discussions, women talk about everything. You can hear comments and questions on most any subject. Raising children and family matters top the list. Such questions as these are common: "I have this problem with my two-year-old. What do you think?" Or, "I'm really upset with my husband. How do I handle this as a godly woman?" Or, "I'm engaged, and my fiancé is doing this, and it's already bothering me. What do I do?"

Recently, I called one of the small group leaders on a Friday night. She was hosting about nine women from Bible study over at her house. They were learning how to make low-fat pizza! The Bible study is called "Life on Life," and that's what we do. We learn how to add life to make meaningful life. It is wonderful to see women love other women. Then, when difficult times come, we can call on each other.

Is that your experience? Are you developing intimate relationships? The Word of God identifies this as the environment in which you will maximize your own development as a godly woman. I am reminded of the recent movie *A Family That Preys*, by Tyler Perry. It was inspirational to watch the friendship of the two main female characters. They loved each other for two reasons: because of their circumstances and in spite of circumstances. God wants you to have relationships like that. He designed you that way. Films that portray genuine, trusting friendships pull heartstrings and show us how it is possible. We were designed for intimate relationships.

WHEN WALLS HAVE EARS

What if people have betrayed you in the past? In the book of Philippians, chapter 1, Paul wrote about the behavior of different kinds of people. His comments offer us insight. From him we learn that people can be opportunistic, jealous, gossipy, and harmful to others.

On the other hand, Paul also noted that some people are genuinely good. My uncle used to tell his children, "There are good people everywhere. You just have to find them." As you seek to develop new friendships, there are some people who will make it difficult for you. Watch out for opportunistic, jealous people. If you don't, when you talk openly, you will later find out that the walls have ears.

As a younger woman, I had a friend who used to call me and talk. I was very busy, but it was a relief to have a girlfriend who would check on me to see how I was doing. Then one day I received a call out of the blue from an older, well-respected woman. She said, "Karia, a dog that will bring a bone will carry a bone. That's all I have to say." That was the extent of the conversation, and I got it quickly.

What she meant was that if someone came to me talking about other people's business, they would take what I said and carry it to another person's ear. Evidently this had been happening to me, and my "friend" was reporting everything she found out about my life! People who lack character when in your presence lack character when they leave you. They will take the information that you share with them and treat it like a sandwich spread—and smear it all over.

If they visit you and bring you information about other people, be very mindful because they are probably observing your home and taking information to the people they told you about. It doesn't matter if they act like they are your best friend.

Just because this kind of people exist (and maybe you have been burned by someone who fits the description), doesn't mean there aren't genuinely good people in the world. It is important that you find and invest in spiritually mature people with whom you can develop healthy friendships. In them, you will see a reflection of Christ as their actions model the example that He set for godly living.

When my oldest daughter was learning to ride a horse, a funny incident happened. She was ahead of me, all strapped into her saddle. Suddenly, she began to slip. Soon she was upside down, feet still in the stirrups, and hanging desperately onto the saddle. The whole family was there, and we couldn't help but laugh hilariously. That wasn't the last time she rode, though. Although it was probably scary for a moment, she continued to learn to ride. Now it is one of her favorite activities.

If you've been hung upside down by someone that you considered to be a friend, don't be afraid of trying to make new friends. Enjoying the company of a good friend can turn into one of the best experiences you can have. The apostle Paul was betrayed several times by so-called friends, yet he still maintained a long list of people with whom he had good relationships.

How do you emotionally recover from relationships with people who have betrayed you? Paul responded to this question from his own life experience. After having been treated badly, he wrote in Philippians 1:18–19, *"What then? Only that in every way, whether in pretense or in truth, Christ is proclaimed; and in this I rejoice. Yes, and I will rejoice, for I know that this will turn out for my deliverance through your prayers and the provision of the Spirit of Jesus Christ."* In other words, Paul chose to be happy and kept his focus on Christ. He valued his friends—real friends who prayed for him.

Finally, this man of God knew that God would turn all of his troubles around in his favor. It is comforting to know when bad things happen to you, you have a God who will reverse that trend and make it good for you. Nobody can put down what God has set up. To get past old pains, develop new relationships based on Christ's example, pray for relief from the pain, and keep the Lord as the primary relationship in your life.

SHARING YOUR DIVINE DESIGN

We were designed for unity in spirit, love, and purpose. Therefore, it will benefit you if you surround yourself with a group of believers who can feel you in their gut and whom you feel in the same way. In order to find these friends, look for people who think like you, are capable of loving you, know how to respect you, and who are not divisive.

Relationships begin in the mind. Some of you have girlfriends with whom you are likeminded. You both love the Lord, and because of that, agree on most things. Your priorities are similar, and you share ways to implement those priorities. Have you ever walked into a gathering, and, after talking with another lady, you found out that she was a Christian? You know that you have something in common. As you begin to talk about the Lord, the time seems to pass so quickly! Likemindedness is the basis of good relationships.

We are to share the same love—love for Christ and one another. When a group of people are of one accord, there is a give-and-take that produces optimal results. The same happens when two people have a genuine friendship; they become soul mates. However, if you find that the love you show to someone is not returned to you, it is hard to trust them. Don't give up on them, though; the Holy Spirit may have placed that person in your path so that you can partner with Him in showing that person what Christ's love is all about. It won't be a waste of time because God will reward you for your efforts.

It is best when you know how to recognize what a true friendship looks like. Any good relationship has a reciprocal effect. Yet people want to get various things out of a relationship. For example, our culture is wealth conscious. Many people will pursue friendships because of who someone else is, what that person has, or what can be gained from the relationship. That is not friendship. That is called networking. It is disappointing to think that you have a friend only to find out that person wanted to use you to accomplish her own selfish objectives. If you wouldn't want that done to you, don't do it to others. Heart connections can be reciprocal; wallet connections are not always that way.

Friendship is also not manipulation. For those who think that they are getting over, they will find no enjoyment in using people to get what they want. This kind of behavior places people in a predicament where they must constantly protect their own interests instead of depending on God to supply what they need. To get ahead, they are constantly looking for ways to impress people.

There is no peace in that. Loved one, if this is you, then let it go. Know that God can promote you all by Himself. Trust God's timing; it is best for you. Save yourself a headache and develop some real relationships—ones where you don't have to manipulate others and be the center of attention to get your needs met.

I work hard and take one day a week off for my Sabbath. When I'm not working, I am having a ball. I enjoy people and love to develop real relationships. I like having someone to laugh with, talk with, and share over a cup of coffee with. I know who I am in God, and I know that He owns me. I'm fine whether He does something with me or not. If He wants opportunities created, He will create them. If He wants me to do something, He will tell me what to do and create a way for me to do it. I'm on His court playing the game that He calls based on the rules that He makes with His ball. That means He is responsible for the outcome.

Ladies, it is so freeing to know that all you have to do is work for the Lord and know that you are not responsible for the outcome. For those of us who recognize this, it allows us to develop real relationships with likeminded people.

What steps can you take to develop friendships? First, get rid of the distance. A little transparency goes a long way. Let people know the real you. Second, if you see someone and think, *I'd like to get to know her,* then work toward the goal of developing a friendship with her. But you will have to give up your reservations. God designed us to live in relationship. Some relationships will work out well and others won't. But none will work out if you don't try. I can almost hear you saying, "But I can't trust everybody." That's true, but you can trust somebody. Sometimes you have to step outside of your comfort zone to meet someone half way.

In writing to the church at Philippi, Paul turned his attention to instructing believers how not to act. He wrote, *"Do nothing from self-ishness or empty conceit, but with humility of mind regard one another as more important than yourselves; do not merely look out for your own personal interests, but also for the interests of others"* (Philippians 2:3–4).

He is saying that we should not act selfishly in our relationships with each other. If the motive behind your actions is to do something and then look to an audience for credit for what you did, your intentions don't amount to much. We all know people like that. If they do something for you, they want to let everyone know they did it so that people will think highly of them.

Clearly, this kind of action is in direct contrast with what the Word of God teaches. We are to act out of humility and consider others as though they are more important than ourselves. How does this look in day-to-day life? If you are a customer service representative, you treat customers the way that you want to be treated when you are the customer. If you treat your customers badly, you will lose in the end because they will go somewhere else. And then you'll be laid off.

If you are a manager, you recognize that your direct reports are as significant as you are. They have the power to make you a success or a failure. If you treat them badly, it will have a negative effect on their performance and in the end will be a reflection on you. How could that possibly benefit you?

If you are the head of a church committee, you need to know that you are not more important than the rest of your committee or even the other members of the congregation. If there were no members, you wouldn't have anyone to help. If you had no committee members, there would be no one to lead.

If you own a company, you should already understand that you are not more important than the employees or the customers. If you are to be a successful business owner, you will act accordingly. We are all part of a whole. We serve each other. We need each other. Besides, God can do what He wants to do without any of us. It is our privilege for Him to love us enough to give us purpose, opportunities, and even our very lives. In turn, it is our delight to serve others for His name's sake. Consequently, others will be delighted to serve us. This is a more excellent way to think and act.

When you do not regard others with honor and esteem, you are not behaving in the way God would have you. Instead, you must willingly and humbly help those who ask you for your help. It means when people need assistance, don't think, *What's in it for me?* Or, *I don't have time for that.* Instead of taking that attitude, you should delegate or do whatever necessary to meet the legitimate needs of others. Pride will make you respond to them in a negative way. Humility will cause you to serve them.

Paul then wrote, *"Do not merely look out for your own personal interests, but also for the interests of others"* (Philippians 2:4). He made very clear that our focus should be on helping other people fulfill their needs and desires. How much time do you take strategizing with another person on how they can accomplish their goals? How can you meet a need in someone else's life? The good news is that you don't have to worry about giving your time unselfishly to someone else and neglecting your own interests. If you do it God's way, He will make sure that your needs and desires are met as well.

If you haven't already done something like this, consider this idea: In my home, the morning of Thanksgiving Day is exciting. It is not exciting because there is so much hustle and bustle in the living room or cooking and cleaning in the kitchen. It is exciting because nobody is home. Everybody is somewhere in the community serving.

Every year, my husband picks a service project. Everyone climbs in the car—and off we go! We have a magnificent morning, serving plates at the homeless shelter or restocking the pantry at the Union Gospel Mission. Other times we might deliver meals with Meals-on-Wheels or transport people to community centers. Later on that afternoon when we gather for dinner, everyone shares funny stories about what happened that morning. Having these wonderful experiences has convinced me that you cannot give without receiving more in return.

You may say something like, "I really don't have time for that. You don't know how hard I have worked or what it has taken to accomplish all that I have done in my life. I pulled myself up by my bootstraps. Nobody really helped me. I had to make it by myself. And make it I did."

The Word says to you that you need to change your mind. Scripture points you in the right direction by saying, *"Have this attitude in yourselves which was also in Christ Jesus, who, although He existed in the form of God, did not regard equality with God a thing to be grasped"* (Philippians 2:5–6).

Through the Word of God, you have to transform your mind by replacing your old ways and thoughts with the example and teachings of Christ. I know what you learned. You learned to toot your own horn and demand respect. You learned to play office politics and corporate games better than other people. You learned how to promote yourself, use buzzwords more efficiently, walk faster, talk faster, and get more done than anyone else. You made sure the buck didn't stop with you. You protected yourself from allowing other people's lack of planning to constitute an emergency on your part. Although you might occasionally accept the responsibility for a failure, it was seldom your fault.

At all times, you maintained the correct posture. As far as subordinates were concerned, you were nice. But since you were evaluated by whether things were done, the people who worked for you had better get them done. If sometimes that took being insolent or aggressive, that's just what it meant. If people thought that you were a five-letter word, it translated into respect for you. You'd try to be nice, but as they say, "it is what it is." If niceness worked, that was fantastic. If not, there was an alternative approach, and you weren't afraid to use it.

It is hard to succeed in corporate America as a woman. Boardrooms are competitive, and somebody always wants your job. So you've played the games and have been successful. But the Word of God says that there is a better way.

The solution to your dilemma is found in the second sentence of this verse, *"Although He existed in the form of God, did not regard equality with God a thing to be grasped"* (verse 6).

If God has given you a position, it is your position because God gave it to you. Everything comes from God. Your position is from God, no matter how hard you worked for it. Your social position is too. There are people who can work just as hard as you who do not have a position equal to yours. You are where you are because of the grace of God.

Know who you are. Jesus knew who He was, and He didn't have

anything to prove. As the Son of God, He was not insecure. He acted unselfishly and gave up His life because He knew that He would get it back (see Philippians 2:7–8). You and I can be like Christ. It happens when we are willing to serve others at our own expense. If you say, "I'm willing. What exactly do I need to do?" The key is found in being obedient. Talk to the Lord, listen to Him, and do what He tells you. He will never direct you in the wrong way and He'll correct you if you do go astray.

Scripture says that Jesus was "obedient" to the point of death. That was His calling. You won't know yours unless you ask Him, "Lord, what would You have me to do?" If you choose to serve God, day by day He will guide you. You will receive the benefit, and the results will glorify God.

You are the daughter of God. Claim your giftedness and be secure in it. You don't have to pull anyone down to build yourself up. Scripture says, *"Humble yourselves under the mighty hand of God, that He may exalt you at the proper time, casting all your anxiety on Him, because He cares for you"* (1 Peter 5:6–7). In your relationships with your co-workers and subordinates, family and friends, learn to serve with humility. If you keep your focus on the fact that God loves you and cares about everything that happens to you, you won't worry about people and situations that come against you. You can be secure in who you are and what God has given you.

The most important thing that you have is the life that Jesus died to give you. After He rose from the dead, He went to heaven and was seated at the right hand of the Father. God highly exalted Jesus and gave Him a name that is above every name (see Philippians 2:9). Because He was obedient to God, He was honored by God.

Ladies, you don't have to honor yourself. You don't have to get credit for everything you do. Be obedient according to your divine design, and God will honor you. Grab the hand of a friend and walk through life together. That's the way you were designed to live.

Minding Your Business: *The Career of a Biblical Woman*

s I was taking my son Ryan to school one day, we were discussing the various forms of business. I was in the process of explaining the different kinds to him: partnerships, sole proprietorships, limited liability corporations, and so on. When I mentioned nonprofit corporations, he broke down laughing. He laughed so hard that he was down on the floor of the van.

Once he finally caught his breath, he repeated my definition, "A business that doesn't make a profit!" Then he started laughing again. At that point, I couldn't help but laugh along with him because he was laughing so hard. But when he finally collected himself, I said, "Yes, Ryan, there are corporations that are not designed to make a profit." He still couldn't believe it.

If you are in business, one of the main objectives is to make a profit. But you also want to make an impact in some way through your work. If you have a career, you have a role in maximizing your earning potential as well as contributing to the success of your organization. In either case, there can be a great deal of work to do in accomplishing your goals.

From the outside looking inward, people may think that achieving success is an easy endeavor. They don't see the balancing act that an individual has to play in order to be successful at what she does. Late meetings often conflict with family obligations. A single mom may have to rely on her mother to care for her children and wonder what she would do without her. A married woman may have to scramble at times to find someone to pick up the kids when she has to work late.

Furthermore, if you own your business, you may have thought that by now you'd have more time to spend with the family. But you can't, because if you don't go in to work, things seem to fall apart. Yes, this is the life you wanted and prayed for. But still, you don't want to lose your life while you build your business.

DESIGNED FOR PRODUCTIVITY

It is true that you were designed for productivity. Your purpose is fittingly found in the Bible, in the book of beginnings: *"Then God said, Let Us make man in Our image, according to Our likeness; and let them rule over the fish of the sea and over the birds of the sky and over the cattle and over all the earth, and over every creeping thing that creeps on the earth"* (Genesis 1:26).

Scripture is telling you that, as His child, you were made in His image. God is intelligent, so you are intelligent. God has emotions, so you have emotions. God has a will, so you have a will. Also, when He made you, He delegated something for you to manage—the earth. When you are running things and conducting business, you are doing what you were designed to do.

DRIVE A HARD BARGAIN

There was a time in the Old Testament that God was preparing to make His children successful. At this particular time, He defined the terms of the deal He had on the table. But, once again, the children of Israel failed to uphold their end of the bargain. Although they were given sufficient warning about how to conduct themselves in times of plenty, they were prone to lose their blessing if they did not meet God's expectations.

When God blesses you, be prepared to maintain your blessing by keeping God's commandments. You will need to study His Word and get to know it personally and follow it closely so that you will know what pleases Him and what does not. God deserves your reverence and a strong commitment to Him; do not forget to honor Him with a heart of thanksgiving. Remember to worship God faithfully and keep Him ever before you. Be willing and determined to do all that He requires of you. In business terms, be ready to drive a hard bargain. Here's the deal:

> *After a meal, satisfied, bless God, your God, for the good land he has given you.*
>
> *Make sure you don't forget God, your God, by not keeping his commandments, his rules and regulations that I command you today. Make sure that when you eat and are satisfied, build pleasant houses and settle in, see your herds and flocks flourish and more and more money come in, watch your standard of living going up and up— make sure you don't become so full of yourself and your things that you forget God, your God, the God who delivered you from Egyptian slavery; the God who led you through that huge and fearsome wilderness, those desolate, arid badlands crawling with fiery snakes and scorpions; the God who gave you water gushing from hard rock; the God who gave you manna to eat in the wilderness, something your ancestors had never heard of, in order to give you a taste of the hard life, to test you so that you would be prepared to live well in the days ahead of you.*
>
> *If you start thinking to yourselves, "I did all this. And all by myself. I'm rich. It's all mine!"—well, think again. Remember that God, your God, gave you the strength to produce all this wealth so as to confirm*

the covenant that he promised to your ancestors—as it is today. If you
forget, forget God, your God, and start taking up with other gods,
serving and worshiping them, I'm on record right now as giving you
firm warning: that will be the end of you; I mean it—destruction.
You'll go to your doom—the same as the nations God is destroying
before you; doom because you wouldn't obey the Voice of God, your
God. (Deuteronomy 8:10–20 THE MESSAGE)

This passage begins with Moses addressing God's people as a
means to motivate them to recommit themselves to God. They were
about to enter the land that God had promised them. It was going to
be a good experience all the way around because God's blessings are
always excellent. On the way to their blessing, these people had been
through a long and terrible wilderness experience. However, God had
been with them, taking care of them and protecting them throughout
the entire journey.

As God's spokesman, Moses was their leader. He commanded the
people to, *"Bless God, your God, for the good land he has given you"*
(verse 10). He said to the children of Israel what I hear teenagers
saying to each other, "You'd better recognize." Even though they had
fought the battle, they didn't have to win; it was God who allowed
them to prevail. Even though He was giving them something very
significant, it didn't have to remain their possession.

After such a long and arduous sojourn, Moses knew the people
well. He was extremely familiar with their ways and knew that they
were very capable of being ungrateful. As a result, he felt compelled
to issue a powerful warning. He wanted them to remember that God
was the source of their blessings. They were not sufficient within
themselves, and he had to reinforce that fact. God deserved to be
continually acknowledged for His goodness; otherwise, the people
would run the risk of being severely reprimanded. Without this admonition, Moses knew that it was possible for the children of Israel, once
they were successful, to forget the Lord their God. He would not
quit being their God, but they could quit acting like He is God.

This happens to successful people all the time. Consider this scenario. The vice president of human resources that you met at last week's power lunch calls you for a Sunday morning golf game. She wants you to fill out the foursome. How often does that happen? You wouldn't want to offend her. But you'll be at church next week. One week won't hurt. The issue is not whether you can play golf on Sunday. The issue is not even missing a service. The issue is who comes first: you, your new friend, or God? Your decision is an issue of priorities. You will invest your time where you expect a reward.

Or try this one. Your friend is having a big barbeque on Sunday afternoon. She asked you to come over and help her get ready. She has invited *absolutely everybody*. You can skip worship today, can't you? Last week it was raining and you slept in. One more week won't hurt. Right?

Once you have reached a level of success in your "promised land," you have more choices because you have more resources to work with. It becomes all too easy to gravitate toward instant gratification. But, self-indulgence can put you in the danger zone. In his list of instructions, Moses put it this way, *"Make sure you don't become so full of yourself and your things that you forget God, your God."* He used the proper noun for God in this passage. It must be known that this God is a specific God. He has a name. His name is YHWH. His name is not money. His name is not power. His name is not fame, nor success. His name is not even your name. His name is YHWH, and He is your God.

Moses told them not to substitute their God for any other god. They needed to beware, because the substitution can happen so very subtly—one decision at a time.

If you have already "arrived," it's never too late to take a lesson from the wisdom of God's Word. Anyone receiving abundance from God can learn a lot from what Moses had to say. Many times the things we go through in our own journey through life are difficult and challenging. We have to make a lot of sacrifices along the way. Yet, we have faith in God that He is leading us somewhere. And in His timing, we will arrive at our destination in God.

The problem occurs when we take possession of the good things we have and start acting like we deserve to finally put ourselves first because of all that it took to get where we are. But the bottom line is, if your time comes, you have to keep God at the top of your list of priorities. This attitude and its subsequent actions will please God and keep you out of trouble.

MORE THAN A CONQUEROR

Some of you are still young in your careers. You have a dream in your heart, and you are waiting for the Lord to bring that vision to fruition. In the meantime, you have not yet eaten until you are full. God may still be leading you out of your wilderness experience. But, know that, if God directed you into creating your own enterprise, by all means, don't give up. Just be willing to listen to the Lord during your journey. He will take you through it and make adjustments to your plan to ensure that you reach the destiny that He has for you.

Moreover, in the interim, don't be afraid of any obstacles that you may encounter. They will come your way, but they will be there to help you become who you need to be. Continue to persist in faith; at the appointed time God will deliver you and bring you into the land that He has prepared for you. Then, after you arrive, you will also need to be very mindful of God's message. Know that He will hold you accountable and expect you to continue to acknowledge Him in your daily life.

On their way to the land of plenty, the children of Israel met with numerous challenges. At every one of them, they were confronted with some obstacle they had to overcome. Although this was a time for growth and development, I imagine it was pretty difficult to stay focused on their goal. They were constantly faced with the choice of whether they would follow God's instructions precisely as Moses communicated them. They were in a situation where the choices they made were critical to the successful outcome of their journey.

Whenever people are presented with choices, naturally they want to make the right one. But there is always the possibility of making a mistake by choosing the wrong thing. Because of this possibility, when we face a roadblock we don't know exactly how to handle it. As a result, we might end up making a wrong choice. Mistakes happen. But keep in mind that when we are following God, He can turn even our mistakes into blessings.

Do you know that there are many inventions that came about when the inventor took advantage of the obstacles encountered along the way? People have set out to accomplish something only to find that they made a mistake. Yet they were not deterred, and that "mistake" turned out to be a blessing in disguise.

So, take heart and don't be discouraged when your plans seem to be off course. God has equipped you to accomplish your goals and the desire that He has placed within you. Find encouragement in the words of Scripture, *"But in all these things we overwhelmingly conquer through Him who loved us"* (Romans 8:37). It should be comforting to know that this is how God looks at you and feels about you.

Adapted from the book *Mistakes that Worked*,[12] by Charlotte Foltz Jones, here are a few examples of inventors who were attempting to achieve something other than what they actually accomplished. Yet, things didn't turn out so bad for them. As you set your mind on reaching your goals, I hope that you will find interesting food for thought in the experiences of others who set out to fulfill their plans.

Post-It Notes

In 1968, Spencer Silver worked for 3M Company and was trying to improve adhesive tape. He discovered the formula for sticky stuff, but there seemed to be no real use for it, so he shelved it. In 1974, Arthur Frye was singing in his church choir and had a problem with keeping his place in his hymnal. His bookmark kept falling out! He noticed Silver's invention and began using it to keep his place. Soon he was using it to write notes to colleagues. Now it is one of 3M's most popu-lar products!

Coca-Cola

John Pemberton, an Atlanta pharmacist, was trying to make medicine. The year was 1886, and he thought he had invented a syrup that people could take to get rid of headaches, sore teeth, nervousness, and exhaustion. He put his concoction in a big kettle over a fire and stirred it with an oar. When he finished, he wanted to sample it. He and his assistant added ice water and thought that it tasted pretty good. They decided to make more, and when they were pouring the second glass, his assistant accidentally used carbonated water instead of ice water. There it was—the real thing!

Frisbee

The Frisbee baking company sold a lot of pies to college students. The pies came in pie tins with the words "Frisbee Pies" protruding from the bottom, clearly visible after the pie had been eaten. When the students were finished eating the pie, they started tossing the tins back and forth between them, enjoying hours of great fun! Every time they would throw one, they would shout, "Frisbee!"

In 1948, a building inspector, Walter Morrison, and his partner, Warren Franscioni, invented a plastic version. When that partnership ended, one of the men, Walter Morrison, invented a new plastic version that he called the "Pluto Platter." The Wham-O Manufacturing Company liked the Pluto Platter and bought the design. The next year, the Frisbee Baking Company shut down, and Morrison was awarded the patent for the Frisbee. He received over $1 million in royalties for his great invention.

Imagine that. Mistakes have a purpose too! When you encounter one, ask God to show you how to recover from it. He can use the mistakes you make when obstacles come your way to help mold you into the image of Christ. He wants you to reach your destiny so He will show you how to navigate through life's choices. Remember, you are not self-sufficient. God is still there for you in the midst of your obstacle course. He is up to something.

As you go through life, first and foremost—rely on God. Then allow for adjustments, maximize your opportunities, think outside of the box, and keep on pushing forward. You will get through your great and terrible wilderness by trusting God to see you through. You will survive the fiery serpents, scorpions, drought, and lack of water. Even when you are eating manna, you are still eating. Keep going and closely follow God's direction. You'll get to the land that God has promised you.

But you might say, "I don't know what to do with my life. I am not a new business owner. I am just starting in my career. What does God say to me?" God wants you to know that when you commit yourself to Him, He will guide you in the path that He wants you to take. He wants you to know that, when you are not sure of yourself, He is with you to give you guidance.

WHAT IS THAT IN YOUR HAND?

What an awesome God. He can use whomever He pleases. That is His plan for giving every one of us gifts and talents that perfectly match our divine design. For example, Moses was the servant that God handpicked to deliver His people from Egyptian bondage. God had given Him this purpose when He created him. God told Moses that Pharaoh would refuse to release His people and that He would strike the Egyptians with many wonders. After that, the children of Israel would leave Egypt a wealthy people.

God gave Moses his instructions, and Moses responded, *"What if they will not believe me or listen to what I say? For they may say, 'The Lord has not appeared to you'"* (Exodus 4:1).

It was obvious that Moses was not sure about the mission that God was sending him to accomplish. God knew that Moses needed some encouragement so He performed several miracles to build up his faith and courage. Here is one of them: *"The Lord said to him, 'What is that in your hand?' And he said, 'A staff.' Then He said, 'Throw it on the ground.' So he threw it on the ground, and it became a serpent; and Moses fled from it. But the Lord said to Moses, 'Stretch out your hand and grasp it by its tail'—so he stretched out his hand and caught it, and it became a staff in his hand—'that they may believe that the Lord, the God of their fathers, the God of Abraham, the God of Isaac, and the God of Jacob, has appeared to you,'"* (Exodus 4:2–5).

God has something for you to do. You need to know your intended purpose and what gifts and talents God has given you to direct your career. Just as God told Moses to look and see what is in his hand, try this self-examination to find out what you have to work with in accomplishing your God-given goals:

What

What physical resources do you possess that God can use? What can you do that few other people are able to do as well as you? What has God already given you as a talent, skill, or ability? What is your passion and interest? What unique experiences have you had that can benefit others? What natural gifts do you possess?

Is

Is there a current skill that you are using? What skill have you kept updated or can be developed for future use? If you could play basketball nine years ago, it may be useful for teaching young people. It is probably not useful for getting into the NBA. What are the current and future uses for your ability?

That

Your ability is recognizable only if you exercise it. Pay attention when people comment to you, "You are really good at . . . " or, "You should consider doing . . . " When you try to do "that" thing, you excel. Sometimes "that" is hidden; it is something you can do that you have not yet demonstrated. Examine your heart. What can you do well? What do you have the potential to do well?

In

According to God's gifting, you already have within you what you need to be successful. You may have to develop your gifting through work, exercise, or education, but God already put in you what He wants to get out of you.

Your

Your calling is a personal discovery; it is between you and God. Don't depend on anyone else to tell you what your calling is and pressure you to accomplish it. God may send people to help or partner with you. But you have to listen to God to develop the vision.

Hand

Thinking is one thing, doing is another. There are people who think about doing something their whole life, but never do it. Certainly, there are obstacles. An obstacle doesn't mean that God doesn't want you to do it. Hear from heaven, and then do something with what you heard.

You have in your hand everything you need for God to perform His miracle in your life. But you may say, "I don't think that I can do it." Then you have something in common with Moses, Samuel, Gideon, Saul, Isaiah, and Jeremiah. When they were chosen by God, they lacked self-confidence too. Just because you don't think you can do what God calls you to do doesn't mean you can't. Your confidence will be in Him, and He will guide you.

Take a look at some of God's leaders, their problems, and their advantages:

LEADER	SCRIPTURE/ BACKGROUND	PROBLEMS	ADVANTAGES
Moses	Exodus 2–4	Rejected by his race; Rejected by his family; Ran away/quit trying; Didn't believe God could use him	Hard worker Curious Obedient
Gideon	Judges 6–8	Weak family; Felt personally insignificant; Low self-esteem	Hard worker Curious Obedient
Saul	1 Samuel 9–31	Lack of impressive heritage; Insignificant family; Felt unworthy	Hard worker Handsome Concerned about others Obedient
Isaiah	Book of Isaiah	Personal sin; Lived in sinful environment; Felt unqualified	Cleansed from sin Heard from God Willing to be sent Obedient
Jeremiah	Book of Jeremiah	Too emotional; Extremely shy; Wanted to be liked; Young; Lacked self-confidence	Heard from God Obedient Articulate

As you study this chart, how many of these problems do you have? Just as these issues did not deter God's leaders in antiquity, they need not keep you from becoming who God has destined you to be. How many of these advantages do you have? They will help on your journey.

The one common trait among all these leaders is obedience. When two of them, Saul and Moses, became disobedient, they were disciplined. Saul disobeyed early in his appointment as leader and lost his position (see 1 Samuel 13:1–14). Moses disobeyed when he was close to finishing his assignment, and he lost his reward (see Numbers 20:1–13). Know that if you have been chosen as a leader, and you become disobedient, there will be consequences.

When God instructs you to get started on your journey, apply the advice of Ecclesiastes 5:3, *"For the dream comes through much effort and the voice of a fool through many words."* Quit talking about it and do something. Take an honest, accurate assessment of yourself. What are your strengths? What are your weaknesses? What are your struggles? What is easy for you? What is difficult? Think about your personality; do you have the outgoing qualities of a salesperson or do you have the qualities of an introvert? Do you like spending time with people or do you prefer to work alone?

Write out your life story. What patterns do you see? How has God developed you? Then get to work on your goals. If God is directing you to start a business, get some help. The Small Business Association has business development offices. They will pair you with a mentor and assist you in developing a business plan to guide you through the startup of your business. Many cities have economic development organizations that offer free seminars to help you get started.

On the other hand, if you want to climb the corporate ladder, you need to find a mentor. That person should be someone who can offer invaluable help as you navigate difficult times. If you need to, go back to school and pursue a degree in the area of your interest or take some classes at a community college to beef up your resume.

The bottom line is, if God has directed you toward a new career, go for it! There are schools all over America to prepare you. Find one that fits your schedule and budget, and get started. If the Lord allows you to grow another year older, will you be a year closer to your goal? Be assured that if God starts something, He can and will finish it. Be obedient and see what God will do with you.

TOO STRESSED TO BE BLESSED

God was getting ready to bless the children of Israel and it was Moses' responsibility to remind them to say "thank you." Children have to be taught to say "thank you." Otherwise when someone gives them a toy, they will immediately start playing with it and forget about the giver. You and I must also remember to say "thank you." When we get a blessing, sometimes we are tempted to say the quickest prayer in the world and immediately start playing with our blessing. But just as any good parent would, God wants to hear us say thank You.

I have noticed that my children draw closer to me when they really appreciate something that I have done. (Don't worry, moms, this habit just started after they were grown!) I recently did something for which one of my children was really grateful. That child kept looking at me incredulously, as if to say, "I can't believe you did that!" I had to keep pointing her back to the gift and reminding her to enjoy it. It took a few days for her to act normally again. God wants that kind of love when He blesses us. He wants us to come into His presence and say, "Thank You, Daddy, for doing that."

The two simple words "thank you" refocus the receiver on the giver. When you are focused on the giver, you remember to follow the giver's rules so that you can enjoy the gift. God has rules for you so that you can enjoy your blessing. If you are a woman, one of God's rules is that you prioritize your home. If you forget that, you will become too stressed to be blessed. You will be working in vain because you haven't taken the time to consult with God on what, when, and how to carry out your responsibilities.

Having conflict at home can negate the joy of your success at work. The way to avoid such an unfortunate situation is to order your life according to God's priorities. You will experience His pleasure and His peace in all areas of your life.

Also remember that negative circumstances will come. They are a part of life. If we dwell on our negative circumstances and forget to be thankful, we will be too stressed to be blessed. If you are so stressed that you forget you are blessed, it is time to refocus your thoughts on the Giver. He is a good God. He is a loving God. He will take care of every situation that comes up in your life. It may not happen in the way that you expect, but when you trust that God's ways are higher and more excellent than yours, He will not disappoint you.

So, seek His kingdom first, and He will give you everything you need (see Matthew 6:33). Begin to order your priorities according to what He has already said in His Word. Listen when He speaks and do what He says. It will help you realize that you are too blessed to accept the stress in your life.

The children of Israel were to bless the Lord for "the good land" that He had given them. One of the reasons for recognizing your blessing and not giving in to the stresses of life is to understand that you have been *given* what you have. It wasn't up to you to get it, and it is not up to you to keep it. The wealth and resources of this world all belong to the Lord, and He gives them to whomever He pleases, whenever He pleases, for whatever purpose He chooses. He is God all by Himself.

But you say, "Wait! The children of Israel worked hard for that land. They bled and died for that land! They lost children and fathers, aunts and uncles, fighting for that land. As far as I'm concerned, I've worked hard for what I have!"

That may be true; but you were still given everything you have. You should know that you must depend on God, because you can also lose it. Even if you've worked for a company for twenty years, you can still get a pink slip. You may have been in business for ten years, but a strong economic downturn or changes in your regulatory environment can bankrupt your business.

People who take credit for what they have achieved don't realize that if God didn't wake them up every morning, they could not accomplish anything whatsoever. The point is, what you have the Lord gave you because He wanted to. It wasn't because you deserved it. It was because He loves you.

Then too, you need to understand that just because you have to fight for something doesn't mean it is not a gift. In fact, don't expect to get your blessing without a fight. But sometimes we can become distracted by a thing that God doesn't intend for us to have. If you are working hard at something but not "getting" what you've been fighting for, ask God if you are fighting for something that He has in store for you. If He assures you that you have, just keep fighting; in the end you'll win.

When God has placed a vision inside of you, use all the skills, gifts, and abilities you have to prepare for it. And the ones that you don't have, acquire them. Just know that if you are fighting for what you want rather than what He is giving you, you may not win the battle. If you are fighting against God's will for you at this point in your life, you will be too stressed to be blessed.

For example, I have a good friend who went to work for a police department. She is a kind, sweet person with an outgoing personality. People love being around her, and she helps anyone that she can. The environment in that particular department was brutal and aggressive. Although she had four small children, she had to wake up at 4:00 a.m. to go to work. After her work day was done, she returned home late in the evening, physically and emotionally exhausted.

When we talked about it, my question was, "Is this the job God gave you? You need to examine His priorities and compare them to the priorities that you have set for yourself. Then, evaluate what this job is doing to you and your family. Does it fit you or God's desires for you?"

Because she was mature in the Word, she had already been thinking about the same thing. Eventually, she quit that position and accepted another one that was more in line with her needs and personality. She is now doing very well in a corporate environment and enjoys going to work every day.

Another close friend of mine is the Public Relations Officer for the Police Department of the City of Dallas. She stands calmly in the most intense situations and speaks the law enforcement's position on the current crisis clearly into the camera. Last year she was named

"Officer of the Year" for the city of Dallas. A single mother, she has worked hard and provided well for her son. My friend is exactly where God wants her to be.

Sometimes it is clear whether you are where God wants you to be. When you have to violate His Word and priorities to be successful, there is something wrong with either the position or what you are doing to be successful in it. God always blesses His plan. Proverbs 10:22 puts it this way, *"It is the blessing of the Lord that makes rich, and He adds no sorrow to it."*

PRIORITIZING YOUR PRIORITIES

When my children were growing up, I made my decisions by one principle: family first. We lived in Texas and had no other family members in the state. My parents were in Arkansas; my husband's family was in Virginia. For our little family, it was just us. Whatever needed to happen, we did it together. If there was going to be a celebration, we had it. If there were decisions to be made, we made them. If there was going to be a vacation, we planned it. There was no grandma or grandpa around the corner or an aunt and uncle down the street.

It was important for our family to have a resource, and I was that resource. I was the "go-to" person for all family matters. In order to be successful in my function, I needed a standard for making decisions. If I had something critical to do, and my children had a critical need, what would I decide? Early on, I determined that I would always decide to prioritize my family's best interests.

It was tough, ladies. I made more sacrifices than I would like to admit. Sometimes I wept because I felt that I would never achieve my goals. Looking back, it is clear that God *gave* me my accomplishments. And because He is a great and gracious God, He gave me a great family as well.

To this day, I don't know why He chose to bless me the way in which He has done. He has given me a doctorate in theology and almost a second doctorate in humanities. He's given me a successful public service career, a successful career as a business owner, and a successful career as a stay-at-home mom. And now, He has given me a significant opportunity to serve Him and you. God amazes me. All of this occurred while I practiced "family first." When God does something, you know He is the One who did it because His name will be all over it.

After conquering land of the Aztec people in the 1500s, Spain sent settlers to what would come to be known as "New Spain." There was a phrase that became popular in New Spain: *obedesco pero no cumplo.* It means "I obey, but I do not comply." New Spain was a long distance from Old Spain. New Spain was just a colony, and it was supposed to follow the orders of Old Spain.

But the settlers in New Spain wanted to make their own decisions about how they would live. Old Spain was a long way away, and it would take a long time for them to even know about, let alone address, disobedience to its governing authority. So the people of New Spain adopted the position of *obedesco pero no cumplo.* They gave honor to Old Spain and declared their allegiance and agreed to follow the orders of Old Spain.

When the Spanish government issued a decree, the people of New Spain would cheer in the streets. They would have parades for the visiting dignitaries. The new colonists would say, "Yes, we agree! We are subject to you, O mighty Spain!" Then after the celebration was over, they just wouldn't follow through. Instead, they went about their daily activities doing exactly what they had done before. They chose to forget that they were only a colony completely dependent on the economic, military, and structural support of Old Spain.

Many of us are like that. We hear a sermon, and we affirm, "Amen!" The choir sings, and we stand and clap. We are deeply moved by the liturgy. We find the stained glass windows inspirational. The readings and the prayers touch our hearts. We participate in the church picnic and the church anniversary. We give our testimony, "I want to thank my Lord and Savior Jesus Christ . . ." Then, we leave church and don't comply.

By what principles do you live? Are your principles consistent with His Word and priorities? Don't allow the priorities you have set leave God out of your day-to-day living. The things that He has given you should never become more important to you than the God who gave them to you. Moses defined the way to know that you have forgotten the Lord: you have stopped keeping His commandments, His rules, and His regulations (see Deuteronomy 8:11). It is a sad state of affairs for you when you have forgotten the Lord and do not obey His Word or apply His commandments to your daily life.

When everything that you have amassed in life is getting bigger and better, this is the time to grow closer to God. According to Deuteronomy 8, you are in danger when four things happen: (1) you have eaten and are full; (2) you have built a nice house and have moved in; (3) you have several businesses that are growing exponentially; and (4) your money is making money and you have a growing portfolio.

When you have eaten and are satisfied . . .

It is one thing to eat and quite another to eat and be full. You may go to a restaurant on Mother's Day and eat a nice meal. But on Thanksgiving Day, you eat until you are full. You are stuffed. You are in danger when your physical needs are fully met and there is no more to be desired. You become satisfied and complacent. You tend to feel like you don't need to depend on God because everything in your life is going so well.

When you have built pleasant houses and settle in . . .

You finally have your dream home, and you are enjoying it. You have parties and invite people over to celebrate with you. This is the way you were meant to live. Your time has arrived. But this is the time when your focus can change.

When you see your herds and flocks flourish . . .

In biblical times, herds and flocks were business resources. Today, your resources may be invested in real estate properties. You may even have more than one successful business and multiple streams of income. When your business interests are growing and becoming more and more prosperous, you have to be careful and take counsel from God's Word—do not be so full of yourself and things that you forget God. He made it all happen for you.

When more and more money comes in . . .

It is nice to have silver coins. But to have gold bullion in a vault is a completely different thing. Once you make one good investment decision after another and begin to watch your money multiply, it can be exhilarating. Just watching those stock numbers go up is exciting.

When your standard of living goes up . . .

Now your money isn't the only thing multiplying. Your real estate holdings are multiplying. You are developing new business lines, and those are multiplying as well. Everything you touch seems to turn to gold. When you reach the point of joining the Forbes distinguished list of the wealthiest people in America, be very careful. You are in danger of forgetting God.

DON'T FORGET

When you are successful, it is easy to get yourself in trouble. You are at a dangerous point. From here you have enough money, power, and influence to destroy your world. What happens right before you destroy yourself? According to verse 14, *"Then your heart will become proud and you will forget the Lord your God who brought you out from the land of Egypt, out of the house of slavery."*

You want to avoid this description of those who have become impressed with themselves and have forgotten that the Lord brought them to their current status. Although you have come a long way from where you began, don't forget how bad it used to be before you started the journey to success.

There may have been a time when you knew almost nothing and felt trapped in your situation. You woke up every morning and hated to face the work ahead of you. You had conflicts, felt restrained, and craved the opportunity to contribute more. You didn't always like the way people spoke to you or talked about you when you were not there. You felt hurt and unproductive. It was the Lord who brought you out of that and brought you to where you are.

When you reach a level of success, keep reminders around you of the journey that it took to get to this point. The wilderness between where you were and where you are now was great and terrible. But God led you all the way through it. Remembering the experience will keep you humble. Scripture says about this experience for the nation of Israel, *"[There were] fiery serpents and scorpions and thirsty ground where there was no water; He brought water for you out of the rock of flint. In the wilderness He fed you manna which your fathers did not know"* (Deuteronomy 8:15–16).

I remember being in seminary and being angry because I had to pay a thirty-five-dollar fee to take a personality test. I was so angry about it that I did poorly on the test. The department called me in and asked about it. I told them how ridiculous it was for me to have to pay thirty-five dollars when I could have used that money for my children. I ranted for about fifteen minutes. Afterward, my questioner just thanked me and dismissed me. I never heard anything else about that test. That was pretty bad.

I remember when our car broke down and we only had one car. I was in school, and it wasn't wise for us to buy another vehicle with one stable income. My husband worked different hours than I did, and his job demanded a vehicle. I would catch a cab to work, walk, or catch the bus home. Because I was too frugal to catch a cab both ways and didn't care for the bus ride, many times I just walked. I remember thinking, "I have a bachelor's degree. I am intelligent. Why am I walking?"

I knew the answer: because my class schedule didn't allow anything else. One day, it rained when I was making my way home. I arrived soaked and tired. I remember asking the Lord, "What in the world are we doing? This is pretty bad." Now I spend thirty-five dollars on lunch, and we have several cars. But I remember the journey.

Do you remember the fiery serpents that you encountered on the way to success? The stings that you sustained hurt you, but they didn't kill you. Some health challenges attacked your body, causing you great pain that sent you to your knees. You remember that near miss; where a decision was critical and you, just by chance, made the right one. You didn't even know that you were trapped on every side, and you still don't know how God pulled you out.

Then there were circumstances that could have destroyed you that quietly passed you by. God moved that one person out of your way. At one time, you didn't even have the necessities of life: food, clothing, and shelter. Suddenly, out of nowhere, God did something amazing. From an unexpected source, God gave you what you needed. You still can't explain how it happened. You remember your journey.

THE EFFECT OF YOUR AFFECT

When you are in the midst of your journey, be encouraged. If God is going to use you, He breaks you first. He has a purpose for what He does in your life, in my life, and in the lives of those He has chosen for His choicest blessing. Verse 16 continues to explain God's reasons for your wilderness experience, *"that He might humble you and that He might test you, to do good for you in the end. "* It is all for your good so that later, you won't say in your heart, *"My power and the strength of my hand made me this wealth"* (Deuteronomy 8:17).

God doesn't want to destroy you. He wants you to know that you can't do it without Him. He wants you to know that you are absolutely, 100 percent dependent on Him—in spite of your journey, your education, your lineage, or your abilities. This is not the end of your journey. Ultimately, He will bless you and give you what He has planned for you. That's why you can rejoice, even in your current circumstances. You can agree with Paul when he says, *"Rejoice in the Lord always; again I will say, rejoice!"* (Philippians 4:4). Choose to have joy because God has, and will, come through for you.

Maybe you are hurting right now. You are reading this book and saying, "I am in the wilderness. I don't know how I am going to make it. Life is too hard." I encourage you, friend, God knows and sees you. He loves you. If you feel like you are breaking, it's okay. God has divine glue; He has a way to put you back together.

One Sunday at church I was looking at the bulletin. There was a picture of a cracked pitcher from which water flowed. I pointed to it and said to my husband, "That's me." I have found that God can use a cracked pitcher. He seems to cherish the cracks because He knows that He is the one who puts us back together. If you believe it, He'll take care of you right now, today. He's developing your faith, and He's teaching you to trust Him. Go ahead and cry . . . and then keep praying. He hears and He will answer. And afterward, girl, you are going to have a *testimony*. His deliverance is coming for you. Trust Him, He loves you.

After you pray through your tears, get up and praise Him. Praise your way into your blessing. Praise your way into expecting God to do what He said that He would do. Tell Him how wonderful He is, how majestic He is, and how capable He is of turning your circumstances around. Remind Him about His faithfulness and His deliverance in times past. Tell Him that you know that *"[He] is not a man, that He should lie, nor a son of man, that He should repent; has He said, and will He not do it? Or has He spoken, and will He not make it good?"* (Numbers 23:19).

Tell Him that you believe Him because He is believe-*able*. He is a mighty God. The Lord will meet you at the point of your praise. When you smile at Him, He smiles back at you. Then you can smile at everyone else. You don't smile because everything is great. You smile because He is great. It is then that people see God in you. Give Him the freedom to show up—and show out for you.

WHOSE TIME IS IT ANYWAY: ACHIEVING A BIBLICAL BALANCE

Scripture presents the purpose for your wilderness: *"You shall remember the Lord your God, for it is He who is giving you power to make wealth, that He may confirm His covenant which He swore to your fathers, as it is this day"* (Deuteronomy 8:18). When it is the Lord providing you with the strength and resources to help you be successful, you won't have to be out of balance to accomplish your goals.

When it comes to thinking about balance in our lives, too often we start at the wrong point. We look at the situations and needs in life and ask, "How do I balance all this?" That is the wrong question. The question you must ask in order to balance your life is, "Lord, what do You want done today?" Your assumption in the first question is that you know what you have to do and you just want His help in doing it. The assumption in the second question is that, since your life is His, you don't know what you have to do and you need Him to tell you. Whatever He tells you to do, He will make time for you to do it.

In practical language, how does that look? It looks like this: Before you start your day, get out of bed early to pray and ask God for His direction. Take enough time to listen to Him. Bottom line, that means you have to learn how to communicate with God. After you talk to Him about your situation, leave sufficient time to find out His perspective.

When you allow Him the time, the Holy Spirit will bring Scripture back to your mind that will bring you invaluable comfort and remind you of His promises. These will be verses that you have read, meditated on, and committed to memory so that you will have them to rely on for your time alone with God. When He finishes, write down what He said. These are your priorities.

But know this: God will do what He said He will do, but only in the context of the kind of relationship you have developed. Don't play with Him. He's God. Prayer is a skill that you have to develop, friend. But you really can't live as a child of God without it. Check what you think you heard against the Word of God. The Word is inspired and God-breathed. God will never whisper anything into your Spirit that is in conflict with His Word.

Here's another way to balance your life; it works every time. Balance comes from implementing biblical priorities. Research the biblical priorities of a woman. Implement them and watch God bless you. If you are on the road 90 percent of the time, and you have children, you are not going to be able to fulfill the biblical requirements of a wife and mother. The reason you can't achieve balance is because your priorities are out of order. By studying God's Word, applying it to your life, and repeating the process, you'll end up smack dab in the middle of His will.

If God is going to give you a successful business, obey Him. You'll get there. He's the One who will give you the business. If God is going to give you a career, be obedient. You'll get there. In the meantime, be careful to maintain His priority in your life—home first.

God will give you what He has promised you as you walk with Him toward His destination for you. If things are not working out right now just the way you want, it is just not the right time. Give the timing to the Lord. There might be some things that God needs to do in you between now and then. My dad used to have a saying, "Patience will untie a knot." Be patient and be diligent in your relationship with God. In His time, it will work out.

The Lord had promised Abraham that He would bless him with many children and they would inhabit the land. Later, when God blessed the children of Israel, He was fulfilling His promise. The question now is, What is His promise to you? Search the Scriptures to determine what God has promised you. Believe God and act on what He says. Let the Word that you plant in your heart be the seed to which your actions will be added so that you can maximize your divine design.

Called Out!
When You Are Called into Ministry

*A*n early church father by the name of Tertullian penned a book entitled, *Introduction. Modesty in Apparel Becoming to Women.* Encouraging women to dress modestly, Tertullian wrote,

> . . . do you not know that you are [each] an Eve? The sentence of God on this sex of yours lives in this age: the guilt must of necessity live too. *You* are the devil's gateway: *you* are the unsealer of that [forbidden] tree: *you* are the first deserter of the divine law: *you* are she who persuaded him whom the devil was not valiant enough to attack. *You* destroyed so easily God's image, man. On account of *your* desert—that is, death—even the Son of God had to die. And do you think about adorning yourself over and above your tunics of skins?"[13]

On a different note, another church father named Clement of Alexandria wrote a book entitled *The One Who Knows God.* He said,

. . . it is possible for man and woman to share equally in this perfection [in Christ] of which I am speaking. For example, Judith
became perfect among women. When her city was under siege, she
went into the enemy camp, at the entreaty of the elders . . . Look
also at Susanna and [Miriam], the sister of Moses. [Miriam] was
the prophet's companion in commanding the multitude. She was
superior to all the women among the Hebrews who were
renowned for their wisdom. As for Susanna, in her surpassing
modesty she remained the unwavering martyr of chastity. She
went to death, condemned by wanton admirers."[15]

The controversy over how women should be viewed in the church
is not new. But Jesus demonstrated what His intentions were in the
New Testament, and Paul helped the church understand how to implement Jesus' instructions.

THE VALIDITY OF THE CALLING

The Word of God points out how women were to conduct themselves in the early church when Paul wrote: *"A woman must quietly
receive instruction with entire submissiveness"* (1 Timothy 2:11).

Unless they were under the authority of the proper leadership, the
apostle Paul then identified two things that were not allowed: 1)
women learning in the church, and 2) women teaching in the church.
This was his reason, *"I do not allow a woman to teach or exercise authority over a man, but to remain quiet"* (1 Timothy 2:12). Paul was a great
teacher; he also represented great authority in his role as apostle.

The man of God wasn't being unnecessarily down on women. He
had a much higher purpose. Besides, there are other places where he
addressed the proper conduct for men in the church. Rather, his concern was with protecting the integrity of the church, and he exercised his authority accordingly. Paul had a responsibility to maintain
order and decorum in the institution for which Christ, our Savior,
bled and died.

A woman must quietly receive instruction

In Jewish tradition, women were not allowed to talk or teach in the synagogue. It was a countercultural idea for women to learn the Word of God, and there were prohibitions against teaching women the Torah. In fact, in Old Testament times, women didn't even go to the synagogue regularly. Some synagogues had a place for them to sit and others did not.

When Jesus arrived, He changed the standard and taught women directly. In the story of Mary and Martha that is found in Luke 10:38–42, Mary sat at Jesus' feet and learned from Him. Throughout His ministry, Jesus supported women's learning and worshiping God. In fact, the immediate reason Judas got mad and betrayed Jesus was because he didn't like it when a woman poured perfume over Jesus' feet and our Lord defended her (see Matthew 26:6–16).

That is the reason why Paul didn't have a problem with women receiving instruction; he encouraged them to learn. But when the women were learning, Paul asserted that they should do so in quietness and full submission. What does Paul mean? In other words, when a woman turns her attention to the study of God's Word, she should have no distractions—just like anyone else.

God's Word must be treated reverently; therefore, a woman should not give herself to arguments, disagreements, or controversy while she subjected herself to learning it. The reason Paul singled them out was that the women of biblical times were to follow the precedent that was set by God in the beginning. As a result, they were to conduct themselves under the leadership and authority of the men over the church. As Paul explained later, it was God who created the man first and appointed him as the spiritual covering of the woman (see 1 Timothy 2:12–13).

Furthermore, Paul had another good reason for issuing this important instruction. It had become common for some women to be misled by false teachers, and Paul wanted to curb this practice of promoting false doctrine in the church.

With entire submissiveness

Paul adds the phrase "with entire submissiveness" to his admonition that a woman learn in quietness. What does this mean? It means that the woman submits herself to the rules and regulations of the church. A picture of full submission is to think about what you expect from your sons and daughters when they live in your home. You expect them to be respectful and do what you say—without an attitude, don't you?

Paul's writing was intended to prevent certain members of the congregation from coming into God's house and spreading a negative attitude. Even today we can find so many reasons to take our focus off God and become dissatisfied with His people. Don't get upset because you didn't get to chair that committee or sing that solo. Don't push your program and create chaos to make it happen or insist on things being done your way. Don't make the church the platform for you to promote your importance. Instead, you must submit to God's order for His church and willingly remain under the authority of your leadership.

Teaching and prophesying

"But, is it proper for women to teach or prophesy?" you ask. Teaching and prophesy are often used synonymously. Prophesying is "forthtelling." When you prophesy, you are speaking the Word of God to His people. Paul was not saying that women are not called to speak God's Word or prophesy. Otherwise, he would have been in disagreement with Peter in his sermon at Pentecost.

The Message Bible quotes Peter's sermon: *"These people aren't drunk as some of you suspect. They haven't had time to get drunk—it's only nine o'clock in the morning. This is what the prophet Joel announced would happen: 'In the Last Days,' God says, 'I will pour out my Spirit on every kind of people: Your sons will prophesy, also your daughters; your young men will see visions, your old men dream dreams. When the time comes, I'll pour out my Spirit on those who serve me, men and women both, and they'll prophesy'"* (Acts 2:17–18).

The call to communicate God's Word is not based on gender. It is based on calling. The prophet of God would not have included females among those who would proclaim God's Word in the days to come. For the purpose of prophesy, God said that He would pour out His Spirit on those who serve Him—both men and women. If you feel called into the ministry, concern yourself with whether God has asked you to communicate His Word, not on the fact that you are a woman.

However, some women are communicating the Word, and they have not been called by God to do so. They are doing it because they want to and not because God called them. If you are communicating God's Word, make sure that God, by His Spirit, called you for this work of service.

We also know that Paul didn't mean for women not to speak God's Word by what he wrote to the church at Corinth: *"Every woman who has her head uncovered while praying or prophesying disgraces her head, for she is one and the same as the woman whose head is shaved"* (1 Corinthians 11:5). Clearly, he would not have contradicted himself. He acknowledged that women could pray or prophesy in the church, provided they are properly covered!

Phillip was a man of God who was part of the early church. He had four daughters who were prophetesses, and Paul probably knew them. During their travels, he and his companions were welcomed into the believers' homes. Listen to one such account when they encountered women who prophesied, *"On the next day we left and came to Caesarea, and entering the house of Philip the evangelist, who was one of the seven, we stayed with him. Now this man had four virgin daughters who were prophetesses"* (Acts 21-8–9). Obviously, Paul was accustomed to women who prophesied.

WOMEN'S LEADERSHIP IN THE CHURCH

Today, there are two popular interpretations of 1 Timothy chapter 2:

1. Some churches believe that when Paul said, *"I do not allow a*

woman to teach or exercise authority over a man, but to remain quiet," he was telling Timothy what *he* himself would not do. They hold that Paul was merely making a personal statement that was not designed to apply to every church for all time. These churches often believe that, if Paul wanted to apply his statement to all the churches, he would have addressed Timothy in the same way that he did the church at Corinth, *"Only, as the Lord has assigned to each one, as God has called each, in this manner let him walk **And so I direct in all the churches"*** (1 Corinthians 7:17).

They also argue that Paul could have specifically said, *"Yet not I, but the Lord,"* as he did in 1 Corinthians 7:10, when he was giving a different instruction. But he didn't. These churches believe that Paul is correcting a practice in the church that had gotten out of hand. The phrase, *"exercise authority"* is interpreted to mean "to dominate," and Christians who subscribe to this opinion strongly agree that men and women should serve in a mutually respectful environment. In churches that interpret the Scripture this way, women are able to occupy most offices.

2. Other churches believe this verse is asserting that women should not teach or exercise authority over men. They believe that Paul's instructions in this verse were not limited to that one particular place or time. Instead, the instructions were intended for all churches for all time. They hold that view because Paul based his statement on the order of creation, which hasn't changed.

Paul wrote the basis for his instruction in this manner, *"For it was Adam who was first created, and then Eve. And it was not Adam who was deceived, but the woman being deceived, fell into transgression"* (1 Timothy 2:13–14). These churches believe that Paul, as the apostle to the Gentiles, had a right to order the affairs of the church. Additionally, since all Scripture is inspired by God (see 2 Timothy 3:16), Paul's instructions in this passage would also be inspired.

These churches point to the grammar in the phrase "I do not allow," (which, based on the tense, means "I continually do not allow . . . ," as opposed to "I do not allow at this time") to determine that this passage applies to God's church in general. Therefore, in churches that espouse this view, you will seldom see women speak or teach from the pulpit or hold primary offices. Women are not allowed to exercise leadership authority. Instead, women are to teach other women. In some churches, a woman may be a deaconess or hold non-pastoral positions.

Your church leadership will have a particular view. One thing is clear, Paul urges women to follow their leadership without creating a mess. That means that you need to accept the biblical direction of your leaders. Don't create chaos. Rather, please God and learn His Word in humble submission.

OUR CHILDREN ARE THE FUTURE

Regardless of your church structure, the Word of God declares this truth about women, *"But women will be preserved through the bearing of children if they continue in faith and love and sanctity with self-restraint"* (1 Timothy 2:15). In His infinite love and mercy, our children will be the ultimate salvation of mankind.

My father used to be the president of the Arkansas Baptist Convention. The convention meeting was held annually during the time around Thanksgiving Day. Every year, my mother would say, "Dear, when these people forget you, your children will still be around. Let's go and visit them this year." Of course, being a preacher, he went to the convention. I didn't mind. I knew how committed he was to his calling. Finally, the year before he died, he visited with my family for Thanksgiving. We had a ball.

The Word is saying to you that, if you are a mother, remember your calling to motherhood. You are investing in the everlasting kingdom of God. Your children will be the Lord's soldiers, pastors, and ministers of the next generation. Don't neglect your children, thinking you are benefiting God's kingdom. Raising godly children who love the Lord, listen to Him, and obey Him will be your most valuable ministry.

THE CHALLENGES OF THE CALLING

As a devoted woman who loves the Lord, you have probably poured your life into your family. When you teach your children, your nieces, your nephews, or any other children who look to you for guidance, you are not only concerned about preparing them for what is to come—you also want them to remember the past.

You point to great-granddaddy's picture and tell them about how hard he worked under impossible circumstances, noting his astounding achievements. You point to great-grandma's picture and tell the children her story, saying, "Look where God has brought us from." But sometimes it seems like they don't get it. You don't want them to forget, because you don't want history to repeat itself.

Well, history kept repeating itself with the children of Israel because they kept forgetting. This was a cycle for them. During a previous generation, they had been in captivity for eighteen years. After they had cried out to God because of their unbearable circumstances, God sent his servant Ehud to deliver them. Ehud killed their captor king and paved the way for the Israelites to take over the country.

With enthusiasm, joy, and the promise of godliness, the Israelites set up their tents. They worked hard. They built a new political infrastructure. They built financial systems by establishing an economic system through capitalistic enterprises. But when a new generation was born and raised in this wonderful prosperity, they forgot God too. It had been eighty years since the captivity had ended. You understand how they forgot, don't you?

Fast-forwarding to modern times, it has been less than forty years since the civil rights movement, but for our children, that period is history. It has been sixty-three years since the end of World War II, and our children have difficulty relating to the events of the Holocaust. How quickly we forget.

The new generation of Israelites didn't remember being in captivity and enslaved to an evil empire. Their priority was the here and now. They did what they wanted to do. This time Ehud wasn't successful in turning them back to God. He was an old man. This was a genera-tion of young people. His words fell on deaf and prosperous ears. God's people were in sin, and it brought God's judgment back on the nation. They found themselves in captivity once again. I can only imagine how Ehud felt. I wonder if he asked himself, "Are they really any better off than when I started this ministry? Have I made a dif-ference at all?"

Sometimes, in ministry, as you invest your life in people and see them making the same mistake over and over, you don't know if your work makes a difference. The problem with asking yourself whether your work has made a lasting impact is that you have become confused. You are evaluating your effectiveness based on the results you see rather than on your faithfulness.

God has called you to be faithful. Your peers may want to hear about your results. "How many people were at your conference?" they may ask. You need to know that they asked you the wrong question. The real question for you is, "Did you obey God in conducting the con-ference? Were you obedient in presenting all aspects of the conference? Did you communicate what God wanted you to say?" If you did, you're done. Let God do the rest.

People are the passion and the challenge of ministry. They behave in ways that are not good for them, and it breaks your heart. You try to protect them. You watch them, trying to make sure they are fol-lowing God's Word. You love them. You think about them all the time. You encourage the ones that need encouragement and rebuke the ones that need to be rebuked.

Looking through lens tinted by biblical understanding and God's love, you frequently see what they don't. You plead with them to listen to the Word of the Lord, since it alone will save them. Some-times they want to be saved; other times not. Sometimes they attack you, even while you are trying to help them. How do you give your-self to them in God's service and enjoy it? What results can you expect?

Chapter 4 of the book of Judges opens with the children of Israel committing sin once again. The passage begins, *"Then the sons of Israel again did evil in the sight of the Lord, after Ehud died. And the Lord sold them into the hand of Jabin king of Canaan, who reigned in Hazor; and the commander of his army was Sisera, who lived in Harosheth-hagoyim. The sons of Israel cried to the Lord; for he had nine hundred iron chariots, and he oppressed the sons of Israel severely for twenty years"* (Judges 4:1–3).

The children of Israel did wrong in the sight of the Lord once again. The Lord saw everything they were doing. The Lord is not blind when the people you serve behave uncomely. The Lord sees the telephone calls made behind your back and the secret meetings. He sees the praises and the criticisms alike. The Lord sees it all, and He has an opinion about it. You are never alone.

After a while, God did something. He sold the complaining, disobedient people into the hands of their enemy, Jabin, King of Canaan. The children of Israel shouldn't have been surprised, but they were. They thought they could get away with their insolent behavior. People who disobey God, even in church, frequently don't expect God's discipline.

Perhaps there are similar instances within your congregation. The children of Israel had been in the land a long time. They had been in charge and running things their way. They were secure in their positions. God had been blessing them. They never thought to question, "Would anything ever really change for the worse? Would God really discipline us?" He did. There are consequences to sin.

For the people whom you serve, there will be consequences to their sin as well. That is why you must tell them the truth. "What do you mean?" you ask.

Ralph Waldo Emerson gave a speech to the senior class of Harvard Divinity School on July 15, 1838.[15] However, his message contained some serious flaws: "Jesus Christ belonged to the true race of prophets . . . . He saw that God incarnates himself in man, and evermore goes forth anew to take possession of his world."[16] Emerson was sending a message that is still popular today. He was telling everyone that God is in them, and Jesus came to point out how wonderful they really are

. . . and how much they can achieve if they realize that God is in them!

God did design us to dominate our environments. We do have the Spirit of God equipping us. But the error in this teaching is that God does not incarnate Himself in man—He incarnated Himself in Jesus alone! Jesus did not come to point out how wonderful we are; He came to address sin. People can only be successful in their life when they address the sin in their lives. Repentance leads to relationship. Relationship leads to success.

First, people must be saved. Second, they must become obedient. We must be careful not to mask worthless theology in exciting words. We must not tell people they are just fine like they are, as if they are already gods who only need encouragement. People must be called to repentance.

When we talk about the message that Jesus brought to the world, it requires the willingness to confront sin, while fully loving the sinner. In the process, someone might get mad at you every now and then. Love them still. When you hold sin up to the light of God's Word, people tend to take it personally. Speak the truth in love—but speak it—for the truth is able to deliver those who will receive it.

It was because of their sin that the Lord sold the people of Israel into a miserable situation. They found themselves in the hand of Jabin, King of Hazor. Hazor was an old enemy. The children of Israel had previously defeated them. But this time, God was on Hazor's side. He allowed them to defeat His chosen people. Jabin was a very cruel king and oppressed the Israelites for twenty years. Old enemies can be dangerous. They may be given an opportunity to harm you when you are disobedient to the Lord.

The cycle of "sin and repent" was a typical pattern for the children of Israel. Ever since the days of Moses' leadership, they had continued to commit sin against God's laws and would later repent. God's servants must be patient in dealing with them because His children today still follow the same pattern of behavior.

Although it is the compulsion of your heart and the joy of your very being, ministry is a life of sacrifice. You give unselfishly, whether people change or not. There will be times when you pray for people who don't seem to appreciate you. Be careful not to follow Moses' example. Moses got angry once when the people were doing their usual fussing and complaining. God told Moses to speak to the rock and it would yield water for the children of Israel to drink. But he didn't do exactly as God had told him.

In anger, he hit the rock as hard as he could and drew attention to himself in the process. That wasn't the message God wanted to send them. They got their water, but Moses died before they reached the Promised Land (see Numbers 20:10–12).

When you have committed your service to the Lord, you don't have a right to represent yourself. No matter what people do, you do not have a right to display your own emotions about it. God wants to deliver people through you. Whatever you do, don't strike a rock in anger when the Lord only tells you to speak to it.

Paul described his position this way, *"I have been crucified with Christ; and it is no longer I who live, but Christ lives in me; and the life which I now live in the flesh I live by faith in the Son of God, who loved me and gave Himself up for me"* (Galatians 2:20). As a believer who has been called to be a leader in the church, the same description applies to you. You're dead. You can't watch out for your own interests.

Your eyes are to be purely on Jesus and what He wants. If not, you will send a wrong message that could tear your local church apart. There will be fights between people who like you and people who don't. They will take their eyes off Jesus because they are so wrapped up in you. Certainly, if God gives you a friend, value her. But remember whose servant you are.

Jesus exercised this principle. He loved His friend and disciple Peter dearly. When Peter tried to protect Jesus and "have His back," he rebuked Jesus when the Lord said that He would be killed. Jesus then turned to Peter and said, *"Get behind Me, Satan! You are a stumbling block to Me; for you are not setting your mind on God's interests, but man's"* (Matthew 16:23). As a servant of God, it is your job to always watch out for God's best interest and His kingdom. It is His job to watch out for you. As the saying goes, you take care of God's business, and He will take care of yours.

HELPING THE HELPLESS

There are special rescue techniques to help drowning people. Untrained people are not advised to attempt to rescue someone who is drowning because the drowning person could pull the rescuer down and drown them. Be wise and position yourself to help drowning people through the proper preparation.

When the children of Israel cried out, God appointed the prophetess Deborah to be their judge. In order for Deborah to be effective, she had to hear from God and know His commandments. She must have spent hours over her lifetime studying the rules by which she would judge. She knew them intricately.

If you are to be effective in ministry, you too must study meticulously. If you minister in a church setting, develop the skill of doing it properly. Study the techniques of people who are well seasoned in ministry, access available training resources, and attend classes and conferences.

Most important, if you share the Word, know the Word. An effective delivery technique is not enough. People may get excited, but how much better off are they a few days later? The objective is to provide meat that will produce growth.

You can be married and called into ministry. Your job is no less important than the married women in Jesus' day who dedicated themselves to ministry. Joanna, the wife of Herod's steward, was a married woman who traveled with Jesus (see Luke 8:1–3). She followed Jesus closely and He didn't send her away.

Deborah executed God's work with focus and commitment. As a married woman, she had the usual responsibilities in addition to the responsibilities of being a prophetess and a judge. Furthermore, we see no conflict between her and her husband based on her calling. If you are called into ministry, there needs to be an agreement between you and your husband that you will be committed to serving the Lord. Know that ministerial work can be extremely demanding.

When the children of Israel were oppressed by Jabin, the commander of his army was Sisera. Although the Israelites knew where Sisera lived, they did nothing to harm him. His army was overwhelming. Barak, the leader of Israel's army, had been told by God to fight Sisera, but he had not done so. Their disobedience had produced a prolonged time of suffering.

Then Deborah called for Barak. Because she was willing to exercise her authority, she asked Barak to explain why he had not done as the Lord had told him. Instead of submitting, this military man issued her an ultimatum. She was speaking on behalf of the Lord, but he was looking at the messenger and hearing it from her only. In defiance, he said, *"If you will go with me, then I will go; but if you will not go with me, I will not go"* (Judges 4:8). Her response seems to indicate that part of the reason that he responded disrespectfully to her authority had to do with her gender (see verse 9).

Prophets and judges were usually highly esteemed and their directions were followed by God's commanders. There were a couple of indications in this case that Deborah's authority was not being acknowledged. First, she had to send for Barak. Second, he showed up with a rebellious attitude. This was a challenge to her leadership. Continue to study Deborah's demeanor and attitude to help you respond correctly when someone acts in rebellion to your authority.

THE SUBMISSION OF THE CALLING

Deborah didn't back down but told Barak that since he wouldn't do his job without her participation, he wouldn't get credit for it. Instead, a woman would receive the credit. Either he disrespected her orders because she was a woman, or she was irritated because he wouldn't "man up." Either way, he refused to do his job in the way that God had commanded.

Deborah was not afraid to be strong when the situation required it. She was able to take charge and execute the responsibilities God had given her, standing up to any challenges to her leadership. When she exercised her leadership, she was a force for the Lord.

In carrying out her responsibilities, she was completely submitted to God's Word. It was God who commanded that they fight Sisera. Since God commanded it, she was wise to insist on His instructions being executed. Deborah did not deviate from God's Word; every action that she took was in line with what He commanded.

Is your ministry in line with God's Word? God has authorized His church to be His weapon to fight the enemy. Jesus said to the apostle Peter, *"Upon this rock I will build My church; and the gates of Hades will not overpower it"* (Matthew 16:18). Jesus paid the highest price to establish His church on earth. Your ministry needs to have a relationship of accountability with the Lord's authorized authority—His church.

If you are in local church ministry, you are responsible for following the direction of your pastor, who is accountable to God. You may not agree with every decision, but you do have to submit to every decision. If there is something that troubles you, talk with your pastor about it. Then if it still bothers you, pray about it. Whatever you do, don't rebel against it.

The pastor is the shepherd and the church is his responsibility. God has assigned you to work with your pastor on behalf of God's kingdom. Even if the pastor is your husband and you are ministering under his authority, it is your job to help implement the vision God has ordained based on the structure that He has established. You are part of God's army. The military operates in strict formation. In the army of God, we must make sure that we submit to His order.

ALLOWING THE INFLUENCE OF YOUR DIVINE DESIGN

You are in a position to influence others. Along with Paul, you can say, *"Be imitators of me, just as I also am of Christ"* (1 Corinthians

11:1). As a leader, you are asking people to follow you. It is a challenge because of the great responsibility you have not to lead people away from Christ. The apostle James proves the point, *"Let not many of you become teachers, my brethren, knowing that as such we will incur a stricter judgment"* (James 3:1). If you teach or communicate God's truth, you will be judged accordingly. You must follow Christ in the strictest sense of the Word.

There can be no area in our life in which we refuse to expose God's truth. If you are not careful, your weakness can be transferred to the people for whom you are responsible, as they follow you. When you ask people to follow you, make sure you are following Christ.

You need to develop relationships in which you will be held accountable. Your partners in Christ's work should affirm when you have done well and call you on the carpet if you mess up. You'll want to find a few people with whom you can be honest. And they are to be spiritual enough to know when you are not.

Ultimately you are responsible for making sure that your worship life and your personal devotional time is consistent with what you teach. Just as in other areas, in ministry it is possible for you to not practice what you preach. You tell others to make sure they have devotional time, don't you? You tell others to make sure they spend time in worship; but in worship, are you distracted? Do you respond to e-mails before you spend time in prayer? How much time do you spend relaxing in the presence of God?

You have a magnificent calling. Enjoy God as He uses you to exercise the influence of your divine design.

CONCLUSION

I have a purse that I really love. It is hanging on a stand next to the desk in my office. My favorite purse has gold handles and the body of the purse has silver, orange, aqua, pink, beige, brown, and every other color you can imagine. There are also studs and sequins of many colors . . . it is so cute! The designer seems to have created it with me in mind.

It matches almost everything! I can grab it and walk out of the house, always knowing that it looks chic!

Whether you favor gold, silver, pink, brown, beige, or aqua, God divinely designed you. He wants to take you out and show you off! He made you beautiful. He loves you deeply. He has filled you up with good works. He has blessed you with every spiritual blessing in heavenly places and equipped you to be all that He desires of you. God Himself has taken up residence in you. He enjoys spending time with you, talking to you, laughing with you, and playing with you. Daily, He watches you, protects you, invests in you, and provides for you.

He has a magnificent plan for your life. He still can blow your mind. So get ready! Be obedient! Your Daddy loves you. You are Daddy's delight!

Notes

1. Langston Hughes, "Harlem," in *Selected Poems by Langston Hughes* (New York: Vintage Classics, 1959 by Langston Hughes; Copyright renewed 1987 by George Houston Bass, Surviving Executor of the Estate of Langston Hughes ([September 1990]): 268.

2. Paper Taffy (formerly Mud Pie Paper), www.moonmippyonline.com, "If the crown fits . . ." Chunky Bow Pad.

3. Jonathan Nelson, "My Name Is Victory!" Integrity/Columbia. © 2008 Integrity Media, Inc.

4. Tina Turner, "What's Love Got to Do With It?" Terry Britten, Graham Lyle, writers. Terry Britten, producer (New York: Capitol Music Group, June 1984).

5. Dr. Anthony Evans, sermon "Blessed Are the Spiritually Submissive," part 4 of the series "Beatitudes, Matthew 5:5," October 28, 2007.

6. Pastor Gerald Brooks at Grace Outreach Center prays this prayer weekly in Plano, Texas. Many have come to Christ through the simple words of this invitation to faith in Jesus Christ.

7. Charles Albert Tindley, F. A. Clark, arrangement, "We'll Understand It Better By and By," 1905, in *Broadman Hymnal*, National Baptist Sunday School Publishing Board, Nashville, 1940.

8. Adrienne Pluss, *"From the Heart of a Woman,"* © 2009.

9. "I Surrender All," lyrics by Judson W. Van de Venter, 1896; music by Winfield Scott Weeden, 1896.

10. Ken Abraham, *777 Great Clean Jokes, A Sparkling Collection of Unsullied Humor* (Uhrichsville, OH: Barbour Publishing, Inc., 2006). Used by permission.

11. Charles Wesley, "Love Divine, All Loves Excelling," in *Hymns for Those That Seek and Those That Have Redemption in the Blood of Jesus Christ*, 1747.

12. Charlotte Foltz Jones, *Mistakes That Worked* (New York: Random House, 1994) 8, 35, 51.

13. Tertullian, *On the Apparel of Women* (Whitefish, MT: Kessinger Publishing, 2004), 1.

14. David W. Bercot, *The One Who Knows God*, by Clement of Alexandria (Tyler, TX: Scroll Publishing, 1990),106.

15. Ralph Waldo Emerson, divinity school address delivered before the senior class in Divinity College, Cambridge, Sunday evening, July 15, 1838.

16. David A. Hollinger and Charles Cappel, eds., *The American Intellectual Tradition* vol. 1, Ralph Waldo Emerson, "The Divinity School Address" (New York: Oxford University Press, 2001), 343.

OUR VOICES

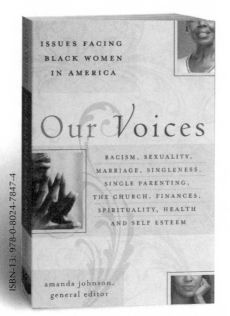

ISBN-13: 978-0-8024-7847-4

What are the key issues facing black women in America today? Does God's Word offer guidance in how to navigate the realities and difficulties posed by those issues? After surveying black women across America to determine which topics are heaviest on their hearts, the contributors of *Our Voices* present a very personal and practical overview. Ten women share their journeys and what they have learned from God's Word about His perspective on key issues facing them as black women. This book provides a powerful challenge to the reader to walk in obedience to God's Word amid a culture searching for truth.

L E V B
LIFT EVERY VOICE BOOKS
lifteveryvoicebooks.com

VICTORY IN SINGLENESS

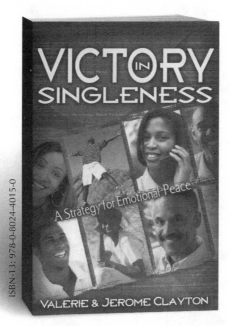

An astounding sixty-two percent of African American women are single! Often these women are saddled with envy, discouragement, and bitterness. Valerie and Jerome Clayton have written *Victory in Singleness* to help African American singles find viable solutions to their real-life hurt so they can become all God has called them to be. Readers will find hope and learn how to develop a strategy for emotional peace by ridding themselves of the baggage weighing them down.

L E V B
LIFT EVERY VOICE BOOKS
lifteveryvoicebooks.com

LIFT EVERY VOICE BOOKS

Lift every voice and sing
Till earth and heaven ring,
Ring with the harmonies of Liberty;
Let our rejoicing rise
High as the listening skies,
Let it resound loud as the rolling sea.
Sing a song full of the faith that the dark past has taught us,
Sing a song full of the hope that the present has brought us,
Facing the rising sun of our new day begun
Let us march on till victory is won.

The Black National Anthem, written by James Weldon Johnson in 1900, captures the essence of Lift Every Voice Books. Lift Every Voice Books is an imprint of Moody Publishers that celebrates a rich culture and great heritage of faith, based on the foundation of eternal truth—God's Word. We endeavor to restore the fabric of the African-American soul and reclaim the indomitable spirit that kept our forefathers true to God in spite of insurmountable odds.

We are Lift Every Voice Books—Christ-centered books and resources for restoring the African-American soul.

For more information on other books and products
written and produced from a biblical perspective, go to
www.lifteveryvoicebooks.com or write to:

Lift Every Voice Books
820 N. LaSalle Boulevard
Chicago, IL 60610
www.lifteveryvoicebooks.com